# The Unreal Estate Guide to Detroit

ᴅɪɢɪᴛᴀʟᴄᴜʟᴛᴜʀᴇʙᴏᴏᴋꜱ, an imprint of the University of Michigan Press, is dedicated to publishing work in new media studies and the emerging field of digital humanities.

# The Unreal Estate Guide to Detroit

Andrew Herscher

The University of Michigan Press
Ann Arbor

Published in the United States of America by
The University of Michigan Press
Manufactured in the United States of America
⊚ Printed on acid-free paper

2015      2014      2013      2012      4         3         2         1

A CIP catalog record for this book is available from the British Library.

ISBN 978-0-472-03521-2 (pbk. : alk. paper)
ISBN 978-0-472-02917-4 (e-book)

"Precisely because physical devastation on such a huge scale boggles the mind, it also frees the imagination ... to perceive reality anew; to see vacant lots not as eyesores but as empty spaces inviting the viewer to fill them in with other forms, other structures that presage a new kind of city which will embody and nurture new life-affirming values in sharp contrast to the values of materialism, individualism and competition that have brought us to this denouement."

—Grace Lee Boggs, *The Next American Revolution*

"The world of capitalist culture, economy, politics, and consciousness ... is full of an incredible variety of imagined schemes (political, economic, institutional), many of which get constructed ... If such fictitious and imaginary elements surround us at every turn, then the possibility also exists of 'growing' imaginary alternatives in its midst."

—David Harvey, *Spaces of Hope*

"The waste of the system, that which refuses proper integration: these are the remains of a commons defeated, and the anticipatory omens of a commons to come."

—Rob Halpern, "Provisional Prepositions for a Project on the Commons"

# Unsanctioned Collectives

# Unsolicited Constructions

# The Unreal Estate Guide to Detroit

# The Detroit Unreal Estate Agency: A Preface

The Detroit Unreal Estate Agency was founded in 2008 as an open-access platform for research on urban crisis, using Detroit as a focal point. Against the apprehension of Detroit as a problem that needs to be solved, the Agency has regarded Detroit as a site where new ways of imagining, inhabiting and constructing the contemporary city are being invented, tested and advanced.

In its research, the Agency has produced an array of concepts to describe and analyze Detroit; tendentiously recovered a series of accidents, false starts and prematurely abandoned projects; and sublimated urgent expressions of longing. This work has been unified by an interest in animating valueless or abandoned urban property by new cultural, political and social desires. Sometimes this interest has yielded experiments such as the nighttime illumination of vacant lots by hijacked electricity; sometimes it has yielded the collaborative mapping of territorial incongruities with licit and illicit community groups; sometimes it has yielded the production and distribution of manifestos, atlases, postcards and other urban texts; and sometimes it has yielded the recruitment of art and architecture students for unreal estate agency via the teaching of studios in institutions of higher learning.

The Agency's program of feral research is an outcome of its engagement with unreal estate; the Agency thereby exists as one of this guide's subjects. At the same time, however, my own unreal estate agency emerged amid the Agency's collective work. The Agency, then, is both within and beyond this guide, at once a context for the guide and a text included in it.

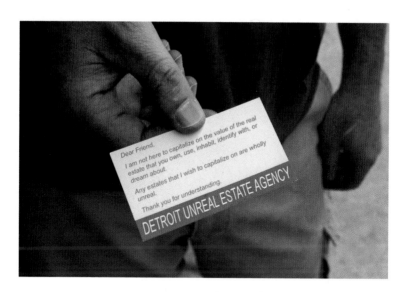

Dear Friend,

I am not here to capitalize on the value of the real estate that you own, use, inhabit, identify with, or dream about.

Any estates that I wish to capitalize on are wholly unreal.

Thank you for understanding.

DETROIT UNREAL ESTATE AGENCY

# Unreal Estate: An Introduction

**unreal** (ŭn-rē'əl, -rēl')
*adjective*
1.      not corresponding to acknowledged facts or criteria;
2.      being or seeming fanciful or imaginary;
3.      lacking material form or substance;
4.      contrived by art rather than nature;
5.      Slang: so remarkable as to elicit disbelief.

Detroit: a city seemingly so deep in decline that, to some, it is scarcely recognizable as a city at all.

And so, to most observers, and more than a few residents, what's there in Detroit is what's no longer there. Theirs is a city characterized by *loss:* of population, property values, jobs, infrastructure, investment, security, urbanity itself. What results is vacancy, absence, emptiness, catastrophe and ruin. These are conditions of the "shrinking city," a city that by now seem so apparent in Detroit as to prompt not verification but measurement, not questions but responses, not doubts but solutions.[1]

Built into the framing of Detroit as a shrinking city, though, are a host of problematic assumptions about what a city is and should be. On the basis of these assumptions, *change* is understood as *loss, difference* is understood as *decline,* and the *unprecedented* is understood as the *undesirable.* These understandings presume the city as a site of development and progress, a site defined by the capitalist economy that drives and profits from urban growth. The contraction of such a site, therefore, provokes corrective urbanisms that are designed to fix, solve or improve a city in decline.

What corrective responses to shrinkage reciprocally pre-empt, however, are the possibilities and potentials that decline brings—the ways in which the *shrinking city* is also an *incredible city,* saturated with urban opportunities that are precluded or even unthinkable in cities that function according to plan. Taking advantage of these opportunities requires an approach to the shrinking city not so much as a problem to solve than as a prompt to new understandings of the city's spatial and cultural possibilities.

Especially in the United States, architecture and urbanism almost always have learned their lessons from cities where the capitalist economy is flourishing, from interwar New York (*Delirious New York*), through postwar Las Vegas (*Learning from Las Vegas*), to late 20th century Houston (*After the City*) and beyond.[2] Cities where the economy is faltering, by contrast, are places where architecture and urban planning deploy what they already have learned. These apparent opportunities for assistance and amelioration thereby provide architecture and planning with precious chances to prove themselves as in-the-know, both to themselves and to larger publics, as well. Relinquishing the desire to repair the shrinking city may thus present excruciating challenges to architecture and planning. It might compel the humbling realization that these disciplines might have more to learn from the shrinking city than the shrinking city has to learn from them. It might also compel the even more humbling realization that *any* specialized kind of knowledge production, whether disciplinary or interdisciplinary, is inadequate to grasp the contemporary city, and that this grasp would have to lead towards a new transdisciplinary knowledge production with a necessarily hybrid, experimental and indeterminate form.[3]

But the shrinking city can teach not only professionals; it also can and does teach its own inhabitants—with "inhabitation" here posed as a political *act* rather than a geographically based *condition*.[4] The shrinking city is neither empty nor populated only by the impoverished and disempowered; rather, the challenges of this city have inspired many of its inhabitants to re-think their relationship to the city and to each other. This re-thinking throws into question the urban ambitions and capacities that the "creative class" has been endowed with, if not arrogated to itself.[5] Most postulations of a "creative class" imagine that group as wholly different—by socio-economic level, by education, and by other parameters of entitlement—from the socio-economically marginal communities that inhabit cities like Detroit. This imagination has allowed the "creative class" to pose itself as the heroic savior, engaged educator, or sympathetic interlocutor of what some have called the urban "underclass."[6] It has also yielded the race-

and class-inflected portrayal of members of the "creative class" as the fundamental harbinger of change in Detroit, a portrayal that has played out in media exposure, access to grants, and a host of other forms, as well.

Socio-economic marginality, however, should be understood not as a call for creative others but as a condition of possibility for the emergence of creativity itself. In this sense, marginality allows for the formulation of new and innovative ways to imagine and inhabit the city. This is not to suggest that the mantle of heroism be transferred from a "creative class" to an "underclass"; it is, rather, to recognize the unique capacity of Detroit's inhabitants and communities to understand and transform their city. Indeed, for many in Detroit, hope for the city's problems to be solved by others has not been relinquished so much as ignored as in utter contradiction to the city as both history and lived experience. In Detroit, that is, urban crisis not only solicits skills of endurance, but also yields conditions favorable for invention and experiment—for the imagination of an urban realm that parallels the realm of concern to urban professionals and experts.

What if Detroit has lost population, jobs, infrastructure, investment, and all else that the conventional narratives point to—but, precisely as a result of those losses, has gained opportunities to understand and engage novel urban conditions? What if one sort of property value has decreased in Detroit—the exchange value brokered by the failing market economy—but other sorts of values have reciprocally increased, use values that lack salience or even existence in that economy? What if Detroit has not only fallen apart, emptied out, disappeared and/or shrunk, but has also transformed, becoming a new sort of urban formation that only appears depleted, voided or abjected through the lenses of conventional architecture and urbanism? *The Unreal Estate Guide to Detroit* is dedicated to exploring these and related propositions and, in so doing, the cultural, social and political possibilities that ensue from urban crisis.

### Properties of Crisis

The guide's focus is a property of crisis termed "unreal estate": urban territory that has fallen out of the literal economy, the economy of the market, and thereby become available to different systems of value, whether cultural, social, political or otherwise. The values of unreal estate are unreal from the perspective of the market economy—they are liabilities, or *unvalues* that hinder property's circulation through that market. But it is precisely as property is rendered valueless according to the dominant regime of value that it becomes available for other forms of thought, activity and occupation—in short, for other value systems.

Unreal estate emerges when the exchange value of property falls to a point when that property can assume use values unrecognized by the market economy. The extraction of capital from Detroit, then, has not only yielded the massive devaluation of real estate that has been amply documented but also, and concurrently, an explosive production of unreal estate, of valueless, abandoned or vacant urban property serving as site of and instrument for the imagination and practice of an informal and sometimes alternative urbanism.

Unreal estate is less a negation of real estate than a supplement of it, located both inside and outside of real estate's political economy. Unreal estate, that is, is neither merely nor altogether oppositional— it opens onto the imagination of positions beyond acceptance or rejection of the market economy. Unreal estate may thus be understood as a term that fits within what J. K. Gibson-Graham calls "a landscape of economic difference, populated by various capitalist and non-capitalist institutions and practices," the latter not simply absences of the former but singularities with their own particular forms and possibilities.[7]

"Private property has made us so stupid and narrow-minded that an object is only ours when we have it, when it exists as capital for us, or when we can directly possess, eat, drink, wear, inhabit it, etc."[8] Karl Marx's critical framing of real estate still points to the seeming unreality of property regarded as valueless or useless. The notion of private property, that is, stupefies us to the counter-values of property devoid of exchange-value or conventional use-values. Devoid of these values, space usually passes out of our cognitive grasp and we become unable to posit a relationship to it.

And yet, the spatial residue of capital's withdrawal—valueless property, abandoned buildings, vacant lots, unserviced neighborhoods—form a system of disaggregated places that can be claimed by and for an informal urbanism that defies the enclosures of private property. The enclosure of commons was a constituent component of the development of capitalism, a means to incorporate collective space into property regimes and profit-making processes.[9] Unreal estate provides a lens through which to see how a decline in the exchange value of property can yield the undoing of enclosures and the creation of possibilities for new sorts of commons—a commons that is neither designed nor intended, but one that is a collateral result of the extraction of capital.

This proto-commons exist in spatial intervals, in the fissures and voids that open up between contracting spaces of investment and ownership. It also exists in a temporal interval, in a moment between the historical failure of modernist industrial production and the possible advent of postmodern urban gentrification. Situated in these spatial and temporal intervals, a commons-in-the-making is at once potential and precarious. It is constantly susceptible not only to further deterioration, but also to further "betterment" as defined by a value regime that equates improvement with profitability. The unvalues of unreal estate, that is, are constantly at risk or even in the process of being recuperated as values—a recuperation that could become part of a process of gentrification, redevelopment or urban renewal.

The proto-commons of unreal estate is also constantly threatened by the least-developed form of capitalism: the primitive accumulation of dispossession, or what is usually identified and experienced as crime. The breakdown of capitalism, that is, invites not only the production of new sorts of values but also the extraction of existent values by force. Violence, of both legal and extra-legal varieties, thus shadows the city of unreal estate; this city accommodates both an alternative urbanism, untethered to the imperative of capitalist accumulation, and the anachronistic urbanism of accumulation by force. In Detroit, this anachronistic urbanism has been emphasized to the point of exaggeration; this guide foregrounds an alternative urbanism in order to allow for more nuanced readings of the city.

## Urban Informality: From Everyday Urbanism to Unreal Estate

Speculations on Detroit's unreal estate have been authored not only by artists and architects but also by activists, anarchists, collectors, community associations, curators, explorers, gardeners, neighborhood groups, scavengers and many others—a heterogeneous array of individual and collective urban inhabitants. The political, social and cultural agencies of these inhabitants are diverse, but their skills, techniques and knowledge are specific, directed and often profound. A concern for unreal estate, then, involves a commitment to the informal production of urban space and urban culture by a wide and diverse range of the urban public. In urban studies, this commitment has been claimed by a discourse that revolves around "everyday urbanism."[10] Translating the concerns of urban informality to the North American city, everyday urbanism has placed a salutary attention on the way that the public co-authors the city through its manifold uses of urban space.[11] Unreal estate situates practices that overlap with those categorized as "everyday urbanism," but these practices invite a rather different framing.

The theorists of everyday urbanism have posed it as an urbanism of the "mundane" and "generic" spaces that "ordinary" city dwellers produce in the course of their daily lives. These spaces "constitute an everyday reality of infinitely recurring commuting routes and trips to the supermarket, dry cleaner, or video store"—a de Certeau-style catalogue of "tactics" apprehended by the public.[12] At the same time, everyday urbanism is also supposed to be a bottom-up urbanism that "should inevitably lead to social change."[13] But this layering of political agency onto the quotidian practices of everyday life produces tensions: everyday urbanism is posed as at once mundane *and* tendentious, at once descriptive *and* normative, at once inherent to a system *and* an alternative to a system. How does driving to the video store inevitably lead to social change? What sort of weakness and powerlessness mark those who rent videos? How do the tactics of the *customer* at the video store differ from those of the store's *employee*? In some of its received versions, everyday urbanism might prompt such questions.

The fundamental forms of everyday urbanism are public responses to professionally designed urban environments; everyday urbanism is thus an urbanism of reaction, whether conciliatory or contentious, to the professionalized urbanism that shapes urban space and life. As such, it does not sustain the progressive political project that some contributors to the discourse want to endow it with—a project that de Certeau was very careful not to attribute to the everyday tactics he theorized.[14] Indeed, the insistent elision in everyday urbanist discourse between "everyday life," on the one hand, and "experience," on the other, points to the commitment of the discourse not so much to alternatives to hegemonic modes of urbanism, but rather to the ways in which these modes are received by their audiences or users. Everyday urbanism certainly offers an "alternative," but this alternative is not so much *critical*, a question of difference from a hegemonic political structure, but rather *authorial*, a question of difference from professional authorship.

Unreal estate is a waste product of capitalism—it is not mundane or generic so much as abject. The urbanism that unreal estate sponsors is less a tactic of consumption, like everyday urbanism, than an alternative form of production. This production can be insurgent, survivalist, ecstatic, escapist or parodic; it can also be recuperative, returning unreal estate to the real estate market. The urbanism of unreal estate, then, can exist in tension with *both* the professional urbanism of architects and planners *and* everyday responses to that urbanism; it is its perceived character as subordinate, redundant or trivial that endows it with its particular differences.

In Detroit, the urbanism of unreal estate has yielded an array of practices, techniques, collectives and constructions. Sometimes—but not always—committed to the extraction of unvalues from capitalism's spatial waste products, this urbanism is also often defined by a number of other common dimensions. This urbanism tends to be improvised, taking shape as unrehearsed and sometimes makeshift moves and actions, as opposed to being planned in advance as a means to a specified end. It tends to dissolve differences between work and play, as well as between art and other forms of cultural or symbolic production, from activism and political organization, through cooking, gardening, caretaking and teaching, to craftwork and social work. It tends to appropriate spaces that appear available to occupation or sub-occupation, or else to furtively occupy spaces that appear to be claimed or otherwise used. The products of this urbanism are often temporary or dispensable and its users and audiences are often limited to its authors or those in their direct company. And these authors tend to be self-organized, taking on responsibilities and functions typically displaced to institutions in functional cities.

The study of everyday and informal practices is often suffused with a desire to endow those practices with resistant or critical force. The urbanism of unreal estate, however, does not mount a critique as much as it claims a right: the right not to be excluded from the city by an inequitable and unjust system of ownership and wealth distribution.[15] Claims to this right run the gamut from recuperative, through reformist, to radical, so that the politics of unreal estate are various.[16]

Occupations of unreal estate emerge from both long-term community activism, short-term artistic interventionism and a whole range of practices that are situated between the preceding in terms of their political, social and cultural stakes. Indeed, as this guide documents, unreal estate development includes escapist fantasies as well as transformative actions; it includes creative survival as well as cultural critique; and it includes the ephemeral aesthetic servicing of those supposedly in need as well as material responses to objective needs through long-term self-organization.

One of the dangers in assembling this unruly set of examples is that it may smooth over the actual and important differences that distinguish these examples from one another. Perhaps the most significant of these differences is that between unreal estate development undertaken by choice, by those with negotiable or flexible relationships to a place and a community, and unreal estate development undertaken by necessity, by those with non-negotiable or given relationships to where they live and who they live with.[17] This guide does not intend to blur this or any other distinction between the projects it includes; rather, the guide seeks to suggest the manifold variety of forms of occupation that unreal estate can sustain by including projects that possess wholly different political, social and cultural valences.

While the urbanism of unreal estate takes place in dead zones for both free-market capitalism and formal politics, this is not to say that this urbanism is apolitical. Rather, it is to assert a distinction between governmental politics and non-governmental politics and to locate the potential politics of unreal estate in the latter—a politics devoid of aspirations to govern.[18] Just like exits or expulsions from the market economy, rejections of formal politics also comprise invitations: to neglect or parody rather than resist, to mimic rather than replace, to supplant rather than reverse. These are invitations to consider political change and political difference not even from the ground up, for "ground," too, is the province of government, but on other grounds entirely, grounds "not corresponding to acknowledged facts or criteria," grounds that can instructively go by the name of "unreal."

## Unreal Estate Development: Crisis as Opportunity

I do not document unreal estate in this guide in order to facilitate its growth, consolidation or protection. Instead, my aim is to investigate the forms and possibilities of self-organized urbanism in the context of the shrinking city. Indeed, if there is such a thing as "unreal estate development," it would not be based on *investments* that pay off in a better world-to-come, whether within or beyond the market economy; it would rest, rather, on *expenditures* in the present moment, critically refusing to mortgage that moment for another, different future. If the development of unreal estate involves an exchange, then it is the exchange of a teleological system of progress, in which the present is, by definition, inferior, incomplete or inadequate, for an ongoing commitment to that present as a site of exploration and investigation. In the frame of unreal estate, therefore, Detroit is not a problem to solve by means of already understood metrics of evaluation, but a situation to come to terms with, in terms of both its challenges and possibilities. In this sense, this guide does not presume to show a "solution" to Detroit's problems; if anything, it indicates ways in which the city is failing better—more equitably, justly and beautifully.

This is not a mere surrender to an environment suffused with social suffering, a bad present that calls out for improvement, whether that improvement be offered by the grassroots labor of artists and activists or by the top-down programs and policies of governments. On the contrary: it is the postulation of the present as a temporary phase within a moralized continuum of progress that allows that present to be tolerated and accepted. The conditions of this temporary present are redeemable "problems" and "failures," subject to improvement in and by a future yet to come, rather than inexorable situations whose values and potentials must be analyzed rather than assumed.

To explore unreal estate, rather than undeveloped real estate, is to confront the complex (un)reality of property that has been extruded from the free-market economy. It is to see the margins of that economy as a site of invention and creativity as well as of suffering and oppression, a perspective that may very well be "so remarkable as to elicit disbelief." The world of unreal estate thus offers a parallax position from which to assess value, an alternative to the single fixed vantage point established by the market economy.[19] In the world of unreal estate, precisely those urban features that are conventionally understood to diminish or eradicate value (inefficiency, inexplicability, waste, redundancy, uselessness, excess) are what create possibilities to construct new values. What usually appears to be the "ruin" of the city thus becomes projective or potential. Reciprocally, the processes that are conventionally understood to support the "renewal" of the city (investment, community-building, securitization, large-scale construction) become, by contrast, banal at best and destructive of unprecedented futures at worst.

Detroit is frequently framed as a city in need: of investment, infrastructural improvement, good governance and many other things besides. And yet, a city in need is also something else besides. Needs create spaces and opportunities for alternative means of achieving viable urban lives. Unreal estate is one heuristic for detecting and exploring these alternative means. Freed from the constraints of free market valuation and development, unreal estate is a site of manifold possibilities of alternative uses, actions and practices. Unreal estate thus opens onto other forms of urban life, culture, sociality and politics—sites at which the city is not only endured, survived or tolerated, but also re-imagined and re-configured.

Such perspectives on urban crisis have begun to emerge in contexts where the urban status quo is taken to be unsustainable, labile or both. For example, AbdouMaliq Simone describes "the double-edged experience of emergency" in the African city—an experience of both crisis and openness, of both challenge and opportunity. With the disruptions that emergency brings, Simone writes, simultaneously come possibilities for new ways of thinking, acting and being:

> Emergency describes a process of things in the making, of the emergence of new thinking and practice still unstable, still tentative, in terms of the use of which such thinking and practice will be put ... a present, then, able to seemingly absorb any innovation or experiment; a temporality characterized by a lack of gravity that would hold meanings to specific expressions and actions ... This state of emergency enables, however fleetingly, a community to experience its life, its experiences and realities, in their own terms: this is our life, nothing more, nothing less.[20]

Overwhelmingly interpreted as a mere urban failure, Detroit partakes of the possibilities brought about by emergency, and, as such, is one among a global ensemble of similar urban sites. In this context, the urbanism of unreal estate is more than just a compensation for "normal" urbanism and more than a response to the lack of formal urban planning. Rather, the self-organization and informality of unreal estate development open onto alternative ways of imagining, building and inhabiting the city. Detroit activist Grace Lee Boggs has thus often remarked upon the city's challenges as conditions of possibility for conceptualizing and producing new ways of living in the city: "the thousands of vacant lots and abandoned houses not only provide the space to begin anew but also the incentive to create innovative ways of making our living—ways that nurture our productive, cooperative and caring selves."[21]

## Unreal Estate Agency

In a market economy, a real estate agent assists with the buying and selling of property; real estate agents act as representatives of buyers and sellers both, helping each fulfill their intention to invest or disinvest in property. Unreal estate requires no such agent: it is not for sale; its values are often obscure, limited or perverse; and it usually does not circulate in a public monetary economy as much as in intimate networks of desire, imagination or shared concern. In compiling this guide, then, I was an unreal estate agent who represented individuals and communities that did not ask for and may not have even wanted such representation in the first place. This ambivalent representation maps onto my ambivalent accountability to those whose work is documented in this guide. I could not presume to share the accountability of the authors of the projects in this guide to their particular neighborhoods and communities. My accountability to these authors is premised not on the ratification of their projects on their own terms, but on opening these projects to new interpretive communities, discursive contexts and disciplinary and transdisciplinary affiliations. This may actually be a form of accountability that hollows itself out—the projects I seek to open up may be destabilized and dislocated by such openings, at least from the perspective of their authors. If so, then "accountability" may become yet another unreal value, impossible to consolidate as simply positive or negative.

My unreal estate agency also extended from the actual to the possible, from the authentic to the imaginary, from the here-and-now to the where-and-when. The unreality of what is contained in this guide, therefore, is various; it encompasses invention of many sorts. My hope is that this unreal estate agency might provoke questions about the "real" existence of what this guide documents, as well as, more significantly, about what the parameters of the "real" are or could be. These parameters ought to invite scrutiny. When parameters of "reality" are passively accepted rather than actively made, all of the ideologies and contradictions that pass as objective conditions of the world are accepted along with them. Marx long ago pointed out that the commodity is a mystification on par with those of the "mist-enveloped regions of the religious world": through the commodity, he wrote, "there is a definite social relation between men that assumes ... the fantastic form of a relation between things."[22] Real estate is the spatial form of this mystification. This guide thus solicits a skepticism toward given models of urban "reality" in order to provoke imagination of the unreal's possible potentials.

The representation of unreal estate in this guide, then, is both partial and eccentric. The guide includes no addresses of the sites it lists and no itineraries to aid the visitor interested in seeing unreal estate for herself. The visualization of sites in the guide favors intensity and evocation over clarity and comprehensiveness. The guide organizes the sites it lists not according to their location or their type, but according to the categories of unprofessional practice, unwarranted technique, unsanctioned collectivity and unsolicited construction. Like the term *unreal estate,* these categories may be supplemental more than oppositional, located both within and beyond their proper counterparts. These categories may offer little in the way of obvious, apparent or useful knowledge; they also may prevent too-easy apprehensions of unreal estate according to received understandings of the city, as well as offer preliminary suggestions for new ways of thinking about the distinctive urban culture that unreal estate facilitates.

At the same time, however, I hope that this guide might partially fill in what is often regarded as empty and abandoned space, space whose only sanctioned future is to be transformed into something else. Such a documentation may act as a friction against many of the schemes that have been and continue to be proposed to save or rescue Detroit. These schemes tend to be predicated on the "acknowledgment" of Detroit's abandonment or emptiness—"acknowledgments" that, at least to some degree, conjure the vacancy they seemingly only point to. What the focus on unreal estate reveals is that these seemingly objective "acknowledgments" are founded on imprecise readings of the city. What appears as empty space from a distance becomes, in closer view, space that is occupied, albeit in subtle, provisional and at times hidden ways.

This guide also offers a picture of Detroit that is in contrast to the picture offered by projects that seek to visually document Detroit's decline.[23] These projects can be characterized by a shared fascination with ruins. Yet some of these projects do not document decline as much as they polemically invent images of decline by proffering the ruin as the definitive urban figure of contemporary Detroit. According to photographers Yves Marchand and Romain Meffre, for example, Detroit is "a contemporary Pompeii, with all the archetypal buildings of an American city in a state of mummification."[24] If the spectacle can be understood as "capital accumulated to the point when it becomes images," then photographs of a contemporary Pompeii can be understood to represent a counter-spectacle, images that emerge from an extreme extraction of capital.[25] Against the counter-spectacle of a city of ruins, then, this guide offers a view of a different city, suffused with potential instead of oblivion.

While this guide is dedicated to a close view of Detroit, it is also a view that is far from comprehensive or complete. If, on some level, this guide maps unreal estate in Detroit, then the map it yields contains many blank spaces, many gaps, many openings to further work and play. The projects that are included here do not form a closed set but rather an open-ended field of investigation and proposition. Much important work that belongs in this field has undoubtedly been left out of this guide. Unreal estate is, by definition, difficult to detect amidst the visually and semantically overloaded landscape of real estate, even in Detroit. If the guide has any effects (which it cannot and should not seek to predict), one might be to focus attention not on what it contains but on what it overlooks: its own failures, whether of theory, history, representation or anything else.

From a wider perspective, this guide is not only an investigation of Detroit's particular condition, but also of urban informality in the wake of capitalist development and, more generally still, the urban culture of crisis. In this sense, it may offer clues for detecting a spatial economy joined to many economies of real estate as a faint but fantastic aura. This is also a guide, then, to many cities that exist on or beyond the boundaries of formal economies, state regulations and public visibilities—cities that are not invisible as much as they are places that professionals and experts are often blind to. These cities exist in a middle landscape between the sanctioned and the rejected; they are cities whose time is both interim and now. Some of the places and practices in this guide, then, may be found not only in Detroit but also in other cities, perhaps including the city where you now find yourself.

## Notes

1. See *Shrinking Cities: International Research*, ed. Philipp Oswalt (Ostfildern-Ruit, Germany: Hatje Cantz Verlag, 2005); *Shrinking Cities: Interventions*, ed. Philipp Oswalt (Ostfildern-Ruit, Germany: Hatje Cantz Verlag, 2006); *Atlas of Shrinking Cities*, ed. Philipp Oswalt (Ostfildern-Ruit, Germany: Hatje Cantz Verlag, 2006).

2. Rem Koolhaas, *Delirious New York: A Retroactive Manifesto for Manhattan* (New York: Monacelli, 1997); Robert Venturi, Steven Izenour and Denise Scott-Brown, *Learning from Las Vegas: The Forgotten Symbolism of Architectural Form* (Cambridge: MIT Press, 1977); Lars Lerup, *After the City* (Cambridge: MIT Press, 2000).

3. See, for example, *Urban Asymmetries: Studies and Projects on Neoliberal Urbanization*, ed. Tahl Kaminer and Miguel Robles-Duran (Rotterdam: 010 Publishers, 2011) and *Transdisciplinary Knowledge Production in Architecture and Urbanism: Towards Hybrid Modes of Inquiry*, ed. Isabelle Doucet and Nel Janssens (New York: Springer, 2011).

4. On the politics of community, see Jean-Luc Nancy, *The Inoperative Community* (Minneapolis: University of Minnesota Press, 1991).

5. See, for example, Richard Florida, *The Rise of the Creative Class* (New York: Basic Books, 2003).

6. On the urban "underclass," see, for example, William Julius Wilson, *The Truly Disadvantaged: The Inner City, the Underclass and Public Policy* (Chicago: University of Chicago Press, 1987) and Douglas Massey and Nancy Denton, *American Apartheid: Segregation and the Making the Underclass* (Cambridge: Harvard University Press, 1993). The concept of the "underclass" has been widely critiqued; see, for example, Loïc Wacquant, *Urban Outcasts: A Comparative Sociology of Advanced Marginality* (Malden: Polity Press, 2008).

7. J. K. Gibson-Graham, *A Postcapitalist Politics* (Minneapolis: University of Minnesota Press, 2006), 54.

8. Karl Marx, "Economic and Philosophical Manuscripts," in *Selected Writings*, ed. David McClellan (Oxford: Oxford University Press, 1977), 91.

9. See Ellen Meiksins Wood, *The Origin of Capitalism: A Longer View* (London: Verso, 2002).

10. See *Everyday Urbanism,* ed. John Leighton Chase, Margaret Crawford and John Kaliski (New York: Monacelli Press, 2008).

11. This translation also reflects the propensity in urban studies to produce theory *in* the Global North *for* the Global North, rather than to theorize the city in terms of global models. On this propensity, see Jennifer Robinson, *Ordinary Cities: Between Modernity and Development* (London: Routledge, 2006).

12. Margaret Crawford, "Blurring the Boundaries: Public Space and Private Life," in *Everyday Urbanism,* 24.

13. Margaret Crawford, "Introduction," in *Everyday Urbanism,* 11. On "tactics of consumption," see Michel de Certeau, *The Practice of Everyday Life,* trans. Steven Rendall (Berkeley: University of California Press, 1984).

14. "The actual order of things is precisely what 'popular' tactics turn to their own ends, without any illusion that (the order) will change any time soon": see de Certeau, *The Practice of Everyday Life,* 26.

15. On urban informality and the right to the city, see Anaya Roy, "Urban Informality: Toward an Epistemology of Planning," *Journal of the American Planning Association* 71:2 (2005).

16. On the various formulations of the right to the city, see Peter Marcuse, "From Critical Urban Theory to the Right to the City," *City* 13:2-3 (2009).

17. On this difference, see Martha Rosler, "Culture Class: Art, Creativity, Urbanism," part 3, *e-flux journal* 25 (May 2011), http://www.e-flux.com/journal/view/231.

18. See *Nongovernmental Politics,* ed. Michel Fehrer (New York: Zone Books, 2008).

19. In this sense, this guide might provide evidence for a critique of what Gibson-Graham call "capitalocentrism": the economic discourse that "distributes positive value to those activities associated with capitalist economic activity however defined, and assigns lesser value to all other processes of producing goods and services by identifying them in relation to capitalism as the same as, the opposite of, a complement to, or contained within." See Gibson-Graham, *A Postcapitalist Politics,* 56.

20. AbdouMaliq Simone, *For the City Yet to Come: Changing African Life in Four Cities* (Durham: Duke University Press, 2004), 4-5.

21. Grace Lee Boggs, "Detroit: City of Hope," *In These Times* 33:2 (February 2009).

22. Karl Marx, *Capital,* vol. 1, *A Critique of Political Economy* (London: Penguin, 1992), 98.

23. See, most recently, Andrew Morton, *Detroit Disassembled* (Akron: Akron Art Museum, 2010), Dan Morton, *Lost Detroit: Stories Behind the Motor City's Majestic Ruin* (Charleston, SC: History Press, 2010) and Yves Marchand and Romain Meffre, *The Ruins of Detroit* (Göttingen: Steidl, 2011).

24. Marchand and Meffre, *The Ruins of Detroit,* n. p.

25. Guy Debord, *The Society of the Spectacle,* trans. Donald Nicholson-Smith (New York: Zone, 1995), 14.

# Unprofessional Practices

**Ruin Harvest**
**Food Infill**
**Municipal Therapy**
**Furtive Inhabitation**

The city of unreal estate is, in part, a city of ruins. These ruins are usually regarded as distressing eyesores or entrancing spectacles; they can also be posed, however, simply as material, able to accommodate new uses. These accommodations are various; the ruin can fabricate something that will amaze, delight or disturb; something that contributes to or detracts from the common good; something that provides respite from other ruins or renders the city's ruination even more intense.

Some ruin harvests are clandestine, their results appearing suddenly and mysteriously: abandoned houses inexplicably painted, one after another, under cover of night. And other ruin harvests are public entertainments: a group of people coming together to watch films projected on the whitewashed walls of an empty house. Abandoned by inhabitants, the ruin is nonetheless occupied by distinct, if enigmatic architectural potentials. Why abandon a building that itself has been abandoned? Why not seize upon just such a building to do something that cannot be done elsewhere and otherwise?

**Ruin Harvest**

Ruin Harvest
# Detroit Demolition Disneyland

In the winter of 2005, Detroit's municipal government prepared to host the Super Bowl by ramping up its demolition of abandoned houses and thereby "beautify" the city. At the same time, a series of abandoned houses in Detroit were painted bright orange. In a communiqué sent to the online site, *The Detroiter,* a group of artists claimed authorship of the project, which the group termed "Detroit Demolition Disneyland." Describing its project, the group wrote that it simply endeavored to appropriate houses "whose most striking feature are their derelict appearance" and foreground them by painting them Tiggerific Orange, "a color from the Mickey Mouse series, easily purchased from Home Depot."

In its communiqué, the group claimed that, through painting houses, it invited Detroit's citizens to "look not only at these houses, but all the buildings rooted in decay and corrosion." This scrutiny, claimed the group, brought "awareness." The precise object of this awareness, however, was left undefined. Abandoned houses themselves? The city's attempt to repress awareness of that abandonment by destroying its most conspicuous examples? The agency of art to critique that repression? Or the limits of art, able to rhetorically critique an urban disaster without proposing alternatives to it? Indeed, while invoking

"action," the only action that the group explicitly attempted to incite in its audience was mimetic: "Take action. Pick up a roller. Pick up a brush. Apply orange." It is just this sort of action, however, that casts the Detroit Demolition Disneyland as an occupation of unreal estate— an occupation that registers a site's deviation from a norm without destroying that very deviation in the process.

Ruin Harvest
# FireBreak

The tens of thousands of vacant and abandoned homes in Detroit have frequently been targets of arson. Sometimes this arson provides a means for property owners to collect insurance on homes they are unable to sell; sometimes it is a means for neighborhood residents to eradicate activities that they deem threatening or damaging to their community; and sometimes it is a form of recreation that is of particular salience in a city where dedicated recreation facilities are scarce or inaccessible.

FireBreak appropriated a series of burned-out, single-family houses throughout Detroit as sites of architectural celebration, performance and provocation. Instigated by Dan Pitera, director of the Detroit Collaborative Design Center at the University of Detroit's School of Architecture, FireBreak transformed burned houses from unusable private property to proto-public space—properties that temporarily sustained public occupations and uses. Some of the FireBreak interventions exploited formal properties of burned houses; in HouseBreath, for example, a house was draped in sheer orange strips of fabric so that gaps in the façade would be accentuated by gusts of breeze and wind. Others exploited the status of abandoned houses as large-scale templates for formal transformations; the Hay House was

created by attaching 3000 rolls of hay to the house's facades. Still other projects re-fashioned abandoned houses as venues for performances or events. The entire exterior surface of the MovieHouse was painted white and films were projected nightly on one of its facades during the course of one summer, while the SoundHouse sheltered a performance by a group of musicians, allowing the sound of the performance to filter out to the neighborhood while visually screening them from the exterior.

In the FireBreak projects, post-arson conditions became objects of investigation, speculation and even pleasure, rather than simply sites of absence or lack. In Pitera's words, "the 'gap,' the vacancy, the abandonment … has become the space of social, cultural, and environmental actions, interactions, and reactions. What is seen as void of culture is actually culturally rich."

Ruin Harvest
## Salvaged Landscape

In Detroit, the city typically clears away the remains of burned homes. In so doing, the city's history of arson becomes visible only through the architectural absences it yields. In "Salvaged Landscape," architect Catie Newell apprehended the remains of one burned house as a resource for new construction; adjacent to the abandoned but iconic Michigan Central Station, this house became both a palette of materials with specific formal qualities and a scaffold upon which a selection of those materials could be assembled, displayed and inspected.

The resulting installation formed a passage into the burned house as well as a construction that emphasized the contrast between the charred surfaces and pristine interiors of the wood from which it was fabricated. While the site and residue of arson are usually regarded as dangerous and unappealing, "Salvaged Landscape" posited this site and residue as raw material for the production of new aesthetic and spatial experiences. The project thereby eschewed "solutions" to arson in favor of attempts to claim, inhabit and exploit arson's material and spatial remainders—a devotion to working with unvalued places and materials that is characteristic of unreal estate development.

"Salvaged Landscape" was also designed to be a piece that could be removed from the burned house it was made from and displayed elsewhere. The facilitation of this displacement registered two conditions. One condition is the city's almost inevitable destruction of burned houses, even when architecturally reconfigured—its inability to recognize unreal estate's unvalues. Another condition, however, is the possibility for these unvalues to become valuable in other contexts—the ever-present capacity for unvalues to be transformed into values. "Salvaged Landscape" is thus symptomatic of unreal estate's precarious existence between actual misrecognition and possible commodification.

*There are many hungers in the city of unreal estate: for memory without anger, for futures worth wanting, for a politics offering authentic alternatives. There is also, still, a hunger for food. The residents of the food desert in Detroit are among the hungry. Providing for themselves in omnipresent liquor stores and corner markets, they make do in ways that, outside the desert, defy easy comprehension. But some take on the ambition to cultivate the desert, converting empty lots into gardens or farms, while others circulate produce on vans, pick-ups or converted ice cream trucks that wend their way through neighborhoods where fresh fruit and vegetables are otherwise scarce.*

*A cascade of activities often accompanies these food infills. Growing food, an act of self-determination, invokes other such acts, from the personal to the collective. The products of food infill are thus consumed in meals that tempt other occasions, from think-tanking and partying to political organizing and community building. Food consumers are thereby offered any number of other identities: gardeners, farmers, food activists, community advocates, locovores, gourmands or hybrids of any of the preceding.*

# Food Infill

# Earthworks Urban Farm

The Earthworks Urban Farm is one of the largest urban agriculture initiatives in Detroit. It emerged from an intersection of two conditions: first, the desire of Capuchin friars and associated volunteers to feed and otherwise assist needy residents in Detroit's impoverished Eastside, and second, the availability of large plots of vacant urban land on the Eastside for non-profit community service activities.

Earthworks was initiated in 1997 as a garden located adjacent to the Capuchin Soup Kitchen. This soup kitchen not only served healthy meals, but also distributed food, clothes and furniture to needy families, provided showers and a change of clothes to homeless people, and offered substance abuse treatment programs, a children's art therapy studio and a children's library.

Originally cultivating produce for the soup kitchen, Earthworks expanded a few years later to a .75 acre site several blocks away, behind the Cleaners Community Food Bank, and began to distribute its yield at weekly markets hosted at Eastside health clinics. In subsequent years, Earthworks also began process produce into such products as canned tomatoes, pickled beets and jams, as well as honey and beeswax hand balm made from bee hives situated on the roof of the

food bank. In addition, it added a greenhouse where seedlings are grown for use both by Earthworks and for gardens of local families, communities, and schools that participate in the Garden Resource Program Collaborative. In 2008, Earthworks began to host monthly community potlucks where food justice issues are advanced and discussion groups with patrons of the soup kitchen are held.

Just like the Capuchin Soup Kitchen, with its diverse assemblage of service programs, Earthworks assembles a diverse array of agricultural programs into a single urban institution. The complexity of this assemblage, indexing perceived social needs, exploits openings in both space (a vacant lot becoming a farm, a roof becoming an aviary) and in time (dinners becoming activist discussion groups and community-building occasions). The filling of these openings creates, in turn, opportunity to facilitate new models of food consumption, community and urban environment.

Food Infill
# D-Town Farm

The D-Town Farm is an urban farm in the Rouge Park neighborhood operated by the Detroit Black Community Food Security Network. The Network was started as a response to a number of food-related issues in Detroit's predominantly African-American population: the lack of grocery stores in many neighborhoods in Detroit; the replacement of home-cooked meals by fast food in many African-American families; and the dependence of those families, and the communities they are part of, on distant others for their sustenance.

The D-Town Farm was developed by the Network as part of a larger project to provide food security, which the Network defines as "easy access to adequate amounts of affordable, nutritious, culturally appropriate food." The farm sits on a two-acre site on the City of Detroit's Meyer Tree Nursery, which the city agreed to let the Network use for ten years. The farm includes organic vegetable plots, two beehives, a hoop house for year-round food production, and a composting operation. Produce from the farm is sold at the farm itself, at Eastern Market, and at farmers' markets throughout Detroit; it is also distributed through the Ujamaa Cooperative Food Buying Club, which the Network also operates. The farm's activities are presented publically in a number of formats, including an annual Harvest

Festival and the Food Warriors Youth Development Program, in which elementary school students at three African-centered schools (Aisha Shule, Nsoromma Institute and Timbuktu Academy) are introduced to urban agriculture.

Through the D-Town Farm and allied programs, solutions to food insecurity have intersected with a range of other issues and sponsored a range of other effects; the farm is a site of community-building, collective-identity formation and political action, as well as agricultural production. The Network's response to food insecurity has thus cascaded into responses to other problems, not all of which are food-related, facing Detroit's African-American population.

Food Infill
# Georgia Street Community Garden

The Georgia Street Community Garden was started by Mark Covington, who grew up in the Eastside neighborhood around the garden's site. Covington began to spend more time in the neighborhood after he was laid off from his job in 2008. His effort to clear garbage from three city-owned vacant lots next to his grandmother's house soon evolved into a project to cultivate those lots as a community garden for the neighborhood, where many families face food insecurity. The garden, mainly planted in vegetables, is tended by both neighborhood children and a network of volunteers drawn from across Detroit and its suburbs; the garden serves as a nexus for the formation of new social networks as well as a new means of food security.

Taking advantage of unreal estate's openness to occupation and re-definition, the Georgia Street Community Garden is also a platform for a variety of neighborhood-based events, actions and initiatives. The garden has thus become a venue for collective children's book readings, family film nights, and public barbeques. It has also become part of a broader project of neighborhood revitalization; the Georgia Street Community Garden Association has acquired abandoned buildings adjacent to the garden from the City of Detroit and plans to convert them into a corner market and community center.

Food Infill
# Brightmoor Farmway

Brightmoor is a neighborhood in Northwest Detroit with large numbers of abandoned buildings and vacant lots. The neighborhood's growth was spurred in the beginning of the 20th century by the nearby development of auto industry facilities; its decline was reciprocally spurred by the post-war suburbanization of those same facilities. As the neighborhood's working-class residents left to find employment elsewhere, their houses were sold to landlords. In weak-market conditions, these houses were cheaply rented, leading to further downturns in property values. In combination with a national economic slowdown, a local epidemic of crack cocaine use, and an upsurge of gang violence, Brightmoor's decline became precipitous in the 1980s.

Around one quarter of all property in Brightmoor is currently vacant. In recent years, some neighborhood residents have come to perceive this vacancy as offering a precious opportunity to self-organize the development of their community. This perception led to the founding of a series of gardens and pocket parks on vacant lots. In the summer of 2009, a consortium of community organizations then began to plan the linkage of these gardens and parks by a neighborhood-scale "farmway." As this farmway developed, it has come to include not only a path connecting around 20 existing gardens, but also new pocket parks,

new community gardens, a wildflower garden, an orchard and a market garden for neighborhood youth. The farmway both joins these self-organized projects to one another and also joins them to Eliza Howell Park, an existing public green space in the neighborhood. In so doing, the farmway has created a neighborhood infrastructure that connects agricultural and cultural spaces, planned and informal initiatives, and sites of food production and food consumption, all taking place on readily available unreal estate.

Food Infill
# Peaches and Greens

In response to the food insecurity that many low-income residents of central Detroit experience, the Central Detroit Christian Community Development Corporation initiated Peaches and Greens to make fresh produce available to residents of the central Woodward neighborhood. Enhancing the neighborhood's access to nutritious food, the project has also facilitated the development of new kinds of political agency and the emergence of new cultural practices.

The Peaches and Greens Market was founded in a former dry cleaners, purchased at a Wayne County property auction. Opened in the fall of 2008, the market provides a place for residents to buy fresh fruit and vegetables at affordable prices; it also buys produce from local gardeners, thereby empowering these gardeners as food producers. In addition, the market was envisioned as a wholesale distribution point where fresh produce could be sold to the liquor stores, party stores and corner markers that serve as primary grocery stores for many neighborhood residents. Recruiting local youth to canvas these stores and establish commercial links between them and Peaches and Greens, the market thereby assists in the transformation of *food consumers* into *food activists.*

The Peaches and Greens Market has been augmented by the re-purposing of a former UPS delivery truck into a mobile produce market. Mimicking the motion of an ice-cream truck, the Peaches and Greens truck circulates slowly along streets in central Woodward, its loudspeaker playing rhythm and blues music and its interior containing shelves of fresh fruit and vegetables. Residents can either flag the truck down or arrange for it to deliver produce to their homes. In either case, produce consumption is transformed into a local ritual, specific to the Peaches and Greens community.

Food Infill
# Field of Our Dreams

Field of Our Dreams is a mobile produce market serving the Eastside
of Detroit. The market emerged from conversations at the Capuchin
Soup Kitchen between artist Nick Tobier and Keith Love and Warren
Thomas, local residents and patrons of the kitchen. Once a week,
via a converted pickup truck, the market roams through Eastside
neighborhoods that are underserved or unserved by grocery stores
and that as a result have constrained access to fresh fruits and
vegetables. Most of the market's produce is purchased from wholesale
produce distributors using proceeds from previous sales; the market
[p.40] also sells produce from Earthworks' Youth Garden, which receives all
proceeds from these sales.

Serving a series of locations adjacent to or within public housing
or other public institutions, the market takes advantage of the
unregulation of both commerce and public space in Detroit. Field of
Our Dreams, however, is not only a market by default, filling a gap in
Detroit's commercial infrastructure. It also suggests the availability of
Detroit's sidewalks and street corners for any number of other interim
uses, from social gathering to informal economies—all equally unreal
from the perspective of the free market.

*Where there is pain, there is an opportunity to provide therapy. Municipal therapists take on pain at the scale of the city, appropriating responsibility for urban repair from the authorities and institutions to which that responsibility has been delegated. In so doing, municipal therapy asserts a right to the city—a right that is often forgotten or even abandoned when urban life functions according to plan.*

*Municipal therapy reveals how the city opens precisely when it fails. While these failures are manifold in the city of unreal estate, so, too, are the therapies that these failures invoke. Damaged homes can be repaired, fallow land can be replanted, space can be provided for exchange, socializing, or remembrance of the forgotten; for any urban failure, or even missed urban opportunity, there is an opportunity for a therapeutic response.*

# Municipal Therapy

Municipal Therapy
# Motor City Blight Busters

The Motor City Blight Busters is a non-profit organization in Northwest Detroit dedicated to "stabilizing and revitalizing neighborhoods." It defines the beneficiary of this project as "the community," an entity with complex and at times contradictory relations to reigning political and economic structures. One component of the organization's ambitions intersects with the city's demolition program, with the Blight Busters employing volunteers and laborers to take down abandoned homes. Another part of the organization's work is dedicated to renovating and building new homes, again with the assistance of volunteers. Among the urban renewal projects that the Blight Busters are in the midst of carrying out is an "Artist Village" in the Old Redford neighborhood in Northwest Detroit, where the organization is headquartered.

The Artist Village takes place in a series of adjacent buildings acquired by the Blight Busters. Spaces in these buildings have been converted into a gallery, café, theater and artist studio, with the aim "to provide a space for artists to nurture and develop their creative spirit ... while also providing a community gathering place where residents of the area could come together to enjoy arts, music and entertainment." The artist studio in the village is occupied by Chazz Miller, who has painted

murals over the exterior walls of the complex of buildings, as well as on a number of other buildings in the neighborhood. Miller also leads workshops where volunteers, many from after-school programs, paint large plywood cut-outs shaped like butterflies, which Miller then places on walls throughout the surrounding neighborhood, including on abandoned buildings that have been boarded-up by the Blight Busters.

The Blight Busters adeptly involve volunteers in the production of art, just as in housing demolition and construction; in so doing, art is entered into the city's sanctioned, if thwarted, development processes. The urban "beautification" produced by the application of painted butterflies to the sides of abandoned buildings becomes a means to symbolically occupy those buildings and assist in their conversion from unreal estate to real estate. This conversion is community-based, but it also advances potentially exploitive economic processes—ways for the community to profit from real estate development.

Municipal Therapy
## Greening of Detroit

The Greening of Detroit is a non-profit organization dedicated to the enhancement of the city's stock of trees and plants. It was founded in the late 1980s as an urban forestry initiative; though Detroit was shrinking rapidly and many areas of the city were becoming uninhabited in this time, the city's urban forest was also undergoing a sharp decline due to the spread of Dutch Elm disease and the municipality's inability to carry out tree maintenance. The Greening of Detroit organized many initiatives to restore the city's supply of trees, from the restoration of parks, through plantings along streets, to full-scale streetscape renovations.

Over time, the Greening of Detroit's interest in urban forest restoration expanded to encompass a wide range of other greening projects. These projects exploited Detroit's many open spaces as resources; urban agriculture was supported by providing assistance to community gardeners and by establishing community gardens on vacant lots; neighborhood tree nurseries were established on other vacant lots; self-maintaining wildflower gardens were planted on lots that the city owned but could not maintain; and infill parks and other landscaped environments were created in collaboration with community groups. The organization also collaborated in the transformation of an

underutilized 26 acre urban landscape, Romanowski Park, into a model urban farm, with community farm plots, teaching gardens, fruit tree orchard and a sugar maple grove.

Through these projects, the Greening of Detroit transformed the vacancy of urban space in Detroit from a liability into an asset. While vacant space lacks value in the frame of conventional models of urban development, it possesses value to a city posed as a site of intense and thorough forestry and agriculture.

Municipal Therapy
## Hope District

The Hope District was conceived by Mike and Lilly Wimberley as a means to develop an impoverished neighborhood on Detroit's Eastside. The Hope District functions as a platform for a series of initiatives oriented around entrepreneurship, self-expression, community-building, food security, spirituality and healing. As such, it eloquently expresses the double bind of wanting to both assist the needy in the world as it is, but also change the world into a more just form. Many Hope District initiatives take place through the appropriation and re-framing of vacant lots: one such lot has become the Little Egypt Open-Air Market, a place for grassroots commerce; another has become the Butterfly Dream Garden, where blank billboards provide places for residents to leave written comments. Other lots have been designated sanctuaries, conflict-resolution zones and places for prayer; still other have become urban gardens growing medicinal herbs, vegetables and fruit trees. The district also includes a building, Club Technology, where neighborhood residents can receive training in computer use, culinary arts and other vocational skills.

The initiatives carried out in the Hope District are conceived as means to consolidate the residents of the district into a community and to make this community self-sustaining and socially and economically

viable. The responses to economic challenge offered by the Hope
District thus do not aim at simply meeting that challenge, but rather at
fundamental transformations of a neighborhood's urban context, social
form, political agency and economic status.

Municipal Therapy
# Navin Field Grounds Crew

Professional baseball has been played in Detroit since 1895. For over one hundred years, it was played on the same site, in the Corktown neighborhood, in a series of facilities: Bennett Park, Navin Field, Briggs Stadium and, most recently, Tiger Stadium. After billionaire Mike Ilitch purchased the Detroit Tigers in 1992, he initiated plans to construct a new baseball stadium, leveraging federal grants and other public funds to realize the project. The new Comerica Park, located about one mile away from Tiger Stadium, was opened in 1999.

In 2009, after a series of attempts to either preserve or redevelop Tiger Stadium, the stadium was torn down, leaving only an open field surrounded by a fence. That field, which still bore traces of the baseball diamond's infield, soon became overgrown. At the beginning of the 2010 baseball season, a group of Tigers fans organized as the Navin Field Grounds Crew and dedicated themselves to weeding and mowing the field and reconstructing the pitcher's mound, bases and base paths. Their groundwork has allowed fans to play pick-up games on a site where professional baseball had been played since the sport's beginning.

The city regards this upholding of baseball tradition as trespassing on city-owned property; while the city tries to sponsor the development of this property, it has attempted to exclude the Grounds Crew from the site. The members of the Grounds Crew, however, have continued to access and utilize what is, for them, a historical site unrecognized by the city. Respecting, tending and enjoying a site that the city merely regards as undeveloped real estate, the Grounds Crew is apprehending that site as unreal estate.

Municipal Therapy
# Detroit Mower Gang

In the city of real estate, public amenities like parks are regarded as luxuries, only to be maintained when the municipal coffers allow it. As Detroit's budget deficit has ballooned in recent years, then, parks have become one of the most vulnerable targets of municipal cost-cutting. In the summer of 2010, the city announced a plan to close 77 parks, comprising around 1,400 acres; while the implementation of this plan was deferred, park maintenance has been reduced to a bare minimum nevertheless.

Public parks, offering space for recreation to all, are never more precious than in times of economic challenge. Recognizing this value, the Detroit Mower Gang was formed as a group of public service vigilantes, dedicated to the upkeep of the city's neglected parks. Acknowledging the pleasure of collective mowing on lawn tractors, the Mower Gang poses its activities as "one part cleanup effort and one part biker rally"; the Mower Gang thus approaches lawn tractor display and riding with all the passion of motorcycle enthusiasts. In so doing, the Mower Gang transforms park maintenance from laborious drudgery to creative play.

Among the spaces that the Mower Gang has tended are O'Shea Park,
Riverside Park, Roosevelt Park and the Dorais Velodrome, abandoned
in the late 1980s and now used for formal and informal bicycle, moped
and go-cart racing. The Mower Gang also collaborated with the <u>Navin
Field Grounds Crew</u> to reconstruct the infield of Tiger Stadium.
Through this work, the Mower Gang renders park maintenance a public
right—the right of the public to care for spaces that it cares about.

[p.78]

*What happens when the occupation of space is illegal, unauthorized or just unusual? What happens when dwelling proceeds without permission or is specifically unpermitted? In its desertion and disuse, unreal estate insistently invites these questions.*

*Furtive inhabitation can be fleeting, lasting as long as a yoga pose is held in a vacant lot; it can persist through the time that trespassing explorers remain undetected in an abandoned building; in the form of a squat, it can last as long as any other form of dwelling. There are vicarious forms of furtive inhabitation, like the seed bombing of an empty field. And furtive inhabitation can remain secret, something that need not be disclosed, publicized or otherwise represented. In the city of unreal estate, neglected and empty spaces can thus be occupied while seeming to remain neglected and empty all the while.*

# Furtive Inhabitation

Furtive Inhabitation
# Detroit Blues

The Detroit Blues are one among the groups that explore abandoned buildings ("urban spelunking," "urbexing") in Detroit. In the group's self-scripted history, its first trip was to the Statler Hotel, where its members pretended to play blues on the stage of the abandoned hotel's ballroom and then decided to name themselves, a white exploring crew, after a musical genre primarily associated with African Americans. With its ironically racializing name, the group inserted itself into Detroit's racial history, a history in which the majority of the city's white population fled in the wake of the late 1960s civil unrest (a depoliticized "riot" to whites and a highly politicized "uprising," "revolution" or "rebellion" to African-Americans). In the context of this history, the Blues' urban exploration became a post-white flight activity—a white fly-over through a now predominantly African-American city.

The Blues' itinerary began with twelve abandoned buildings in downtown Detroit. In a 2004 article in the *Detroit Free Press,* these buildings were termed "Towers of Neglect" in drastic need of renovation. The Blues re-conceptualized these buildings as the "Dirty Dozen," key destinations of urban exploration in Detroit. In so doing, the group appropriated the abandonment and decay of the buildings as

positive values enhancing the experience of trespassing within them. This was an aestheticization of abandonment and decay, but one that stands in opposition to the aestheticization of occupation and growth that drives urban development.

In the group's self-understanding, however, urban exploration is voided of all utility except that of affordable leisure: free entertainment for free time. The exploration of abandoned buildings, that is, becomes a kind of *budget blight tourism,* with the conditions of blight registered not only by the destinations of exploration, but also by the form of exploration itself.

Furtive Inhabitation
# Hookie Monsters

Abandoned schools are prominent landmarks in Detroit's cityscape. They are outcomes not only of declining student enrollments but also of the city's strategy to cope with the school budget deficits that these declines cause: as the city closes schools and raises class size to reduce costs, more students are driven out of the public school system, necessitating still more school closures.

The ejection of school buildings from the system of formal education also makes these buildings available for alternative forms of self-organized education. The Hookie Monsters are an urban exploration crew whose trips began as investigations of the architectural residue of school closures. These investigations posited Detroit's abandoned schools as an abject heritage as worthy of attention as those inheritances from the past that the city frames as such.

Branching out to explore abandoned architecture of many types, the Monsters have opened a new perspective on sites that tend to be either ignored as devoid of historical interest or visualized as sublime ruins. For the Monsters, the abandoned building is a *counter-public space*—a site that can accommodate those whose identities and interests are

not socially valorized. The exploration of these sites thus offers a way to occupy the city according to self-generated codes and conventions.

In February 2011, Detroit's Emergency Financial Manager announced a plan to close half of the city's remaining 144 schools and consolidate students into the remaining schools by increasing maximum class size to 60 students. If implemented, this devastating blow to the city's public education system will also open up a number of new sites to explorations like those undertaken by the Monsters.

Furtive Inhabitation
## Urban Yoga Lab

In the summer of 2007, a group of Detroit-based yoga adepts, aficionados, poseurs and wannabes self-constituted as the Urban Yoga Lab and began to stage clandestine yoga sessions in decrepit urban spaces around the city. At each session, the group developed new yoga positions in response to the particular formal, visual and emotional qualities of the space it occupied. In so doing, the group claimed to extricate yoga practice from its post-modern context of physical and spiritual fitness and return to that practice as a means of "conjoining" or "unifying" subject and object into oneness, as yoga was originally constituted.

The vivid and strange spaces of Detroit, according to the Lab, can prompt new forms of urban subjectivity; the yoga practice the Lab is evolving is intended to provide one entry to that subjectivity. At the same time, the members of the Lab seek to position yoga practice not as a therapeutic response to personal suffering, as is often done, but rather as a way to access landscapes that society's privileged members usually encounter only under duress. The access to these landscapes provided by urban yoga is metaphorical and deliberate, rather than actual and forced; at the same time, however, it opens onto other accesses whose targets and consequences cannot be predicted in advance.

Furtive Inhabitation
## Seed Detroit

In Seed Detroit, wildflowers were planted on some of the many vacant lots in the Brush Park District. This planting did not "improve" these lots so much as foreground them as distinctive spaces providing unique sights, smells and sounds to city dwellers. Surfaced with wildflowers, vacant lots were thus re-framed as "urban prairies." This re-framing was accomplished by *flower tagging*—marking a surface with flowers in order to render that surface visible in a new way.

By using wildflowers as its tagging instrument, Seed Detroit turned planting into an easily accomplished act. Wildflowers seeds were placed in envelopes left on signs posted at vacant lots; instructions directed participants to simply tear an envelope open and sprinkle the seeds within on the lot. While involving the public in planting, this involvement required a minimum investment of time and energy; Seed Detroit created an *uncommitted community* only unified by its brief participation in acts of seed bombing.

# Unwarranted Techniques

**Feral Research**
**Waste Curation**
**Public Secrecy**
**Radical Hospitality**

*To study unreal estate while participating in its unreality requires feral research—an improvised and provisional study of an improvised and provisional city. Feral research is devoid of commitment to a discipline; it is dedicated to the exploitation of circumstances rather than to the extension of a formalized body of knowledge. Feral research promises neither contributions nor predictable outcomes; opportunistic and tactical, the feral researcher makes it up as she goes.*

*The feral researcher can move stealthily through the city, incognito and unannounced, or loiter, waiting for something to happen, or stalk, devoting obsessive attention to her object of interest. The outcomes of feral research are as various as its processes: these outcomes can disappear amidst the city's surfaces and spaces, or be misrecognized as mere aesthetic play, or, worst of all, devalued as an inferior form of "authentic research." Feral research will, then, never be proposed for peer review; its evaluation will always rest on stakes that it has to invent for itself.*

# Feral Research

# Detroit Geographical Expedition

In 1968, radical Detroit geographer William Bunge founded the Detroit Geographical Expedition. The Expedition was a platform to produce a new sort of spatial knowledge—neither disciplinary nor professional knowledge, but knowledge that could serve as a resource for Detroit and, most especially, for the city's disenfranchised African-American population. For two years, Bunge and his students at Wayne State University collaborated with Detroit activists and residents to expose the spatial effects of racism, disinvestment and impoverishment in the city. Then, in still-mysterious circumstances, Bunge either resigned or was fired from his position in Wayne State's Department of Geography in 1970 and the Expedition disbanded.

The four reports of the Expedition were never published, but copies of these reports were archived in the Map Collection of the University of Michigan Graduate Library in Ann Arbor. In 2009, a group of Michigan architecture students found these reports in the course of conducting research on Detroit. Inspired by the Expedition's ambitions, the students re-founded the Expedition and attempted to continue Bunge's effort to produce "maps that could change the map of the world."

Based on the family connections of one of its members, the Expedition initiated a collaboration with residents of an Eastside neighborhood and began a project to map that neighborhood's spaces of insecurity. Over the next 18 months, the project developed into a complex atlas documenting a series of spatial conditions, events and practices in and around the neighborhood. Following the precepts of the original Expedition, this documentation was founded on the urban knowledge and experience of the city's marginalized communities, groups and individuals.

As the Expedition's atlas was being prepared for publication, a crack house whose location was documented in the publication was burned, probably by neighborhood residents. Members of the Expedition split over their interpretation of this burning; most thought it represented an unwelcome extension of their research while a few thought it was one of the most profound ways that this research could be put into practice. This split subverted the atlas project but also led to the Expedition taking new form as a laboratory for urban advocacy.

Feral Research
# Pink Pony Express

The Pink Pony Express is a research collaborative investigating small-scale urban initiatives in Detroit. The basic strategy of the Ponies is *research through making,* with every exploration taking material form. These forms occupy or are brought back to the places under study, so that the practice of the Ponies includes a kind of "giving back" to the communities they live and work in. What the Ponies return, however, may not be immediately recognizable to the members of those communities; their work *gives back what was never possessed in the first place,* with research thus becoming an occasion for generous and eccentric exchange.

[p.56] In one typical project, the Ponies mapped the itinerary of the <u>Peaches and Greens</u> produce truck as it sold fresh fruit and vegetables to liquor stores and on street corners in Highland Park. Rather than producing a literal map, however, the Ponies made a still-life tableau of all the fruit and vegetables sold in one day, photographed the tableau on Belle Isle, made pies and tarts with the assembled produce, and then gave those baked goods away at the <u>Peaches and Greens</u> market. The Ponies also have experimented with cooking on manhole covers heated by steam from Detroit's controversial municipal incinerator; broadcasting messages of urban possibility on Christian ministry radio shows,

112

Sunday church services and church message boards; and physically
[p.194] mapping social networks on a block of <u>Farnsworth Street</u>. By returning,
in various ways, the results of these experiments to members of the
relevant communities, the Pink Pony Express enters the world of unreal
estate instead of merely producing commentary on that world from a
position of presumed distance.

*The city in crisis is a city of loss, but also a city of gain: in ruined buildings, in the flora and fauna of abandoned landscapes, in the detritus that gathers where homes and neighborhoods are forsaken. What's left behind and left unattended are waste products, but only in a conventional sense; they are also perverse treasures, available to eccentric forms of care.*

*Waste curation seizes on the products of post-industrial decay. These products can be curated by endowing them with new forms—the "ghetto palm" that colonizes ground around abandoned buildings offers wood for the crafting of furniture, the berry bushes that grow on vacant lots offer fruit for scavenging and jamming. Curation can also involve the circulation of detritus from one site, where it is useless, to another site, where it assumes new functions—the doors, windows and ornaments of abandoned buildings taken to buildings under construction or reconstruction. These techniques are drastically sustainable—waste curation is a technique for sustainability in drastic circumstances.*

# Waste Curation

# Tree of Heaven Woodshop

The Tree of Heaven Woodshop was founded by Mitch Cope, Ingo
Vetter and Annette Weisser as a collective of artists, craftspeople
and researchers who work with wood from the *Ailanthus altissima*, or
"tree of heaven," the English translation of the tree's Chinese name.
The "tree of heaven" is a rapidly growing and aggressively spreading
deciduous tree that easily withstands polluted soil; able to colonize
areas that other plants and trees cannot tolerate, it is found in, on
and around abandoned buildings throughout Detroit. Conventionally
regarded as a sign of post-industrial decay, the "tree of heaven" is
posed by the Woodshop as, conversely, a post-industrial resource with
its own unique qualities and values. According to the Woodshop, these
qualities and values can refract from the "tree of heaven" to Detroit,
whose signs of blight and ruination can also become materials for new
forms of production.

The Tree of Heaven Woodshop stages its harvesting and processing
of lumber in Detroit as an "absurd performance"—a performance
that acknowledges the city's existing condition through a complex
admixture of celebration, parody, mourning and pragmatic use. These
performances yield objects that are custom-made for exhibitions
or galleries. The objects are, in the words of the workshop, "highly

rhetorical"; their function is not simply to be used as equipment or furniture, but to communicate aspects of their urban site of origin. The Tree of Heaven Woodshop suggests an innovative kind of sustainable economy, one which is premised not on transforming Detroit into a recognizably renewed city, but on recognizing and responding to the city's particular condition in the present.

## Architectural Salvage Warehouse

The building demolitions that are widespread in Detroit typically yield debris destined for landfills and dumps. The Architectural Salvage Warehouse is a non-profit organization that has apprehended building demolition as an opportunity to salvage and reuse architectural material, create skilled jobs, augment historic preservation practice and enhance environmental sustainability. As alternatives to demolition, the Warehouse offers *deconstruction,* the systematic disassembly of buildings into reusable parts, and *skimming,* the capture of easy-to-remove building components such as doors, windows and fixtures. The Warehouse trains workers in these practices, which then yield materials that are offered for purchase at its retail store.

Through deconstruction and skimming, the Warehouse transforms building demolition from an end point, the terminal moment in the life of a building, into a point of transition, a moment when a building's materials leave one site and become available to other sites, other architecture and other purposes. Moreover, the articulation of this transition as an opportunity for a specific sort of labor practice, environmental awareness, and historical consciousness adds values to what would otherwise be a mere reaction to value's absence.

# Friends of Gorgeous Berries

Among the plants that flourish on vacant lots in Detroit are mulberry trees and blackberry bushes, both native to the region. In the summer, these plants, located on abandoned and rarely visited property, produce huge quantities of fruit that often remains unharvested. The Friends of Gorgeous Berries is an urban gleaning project focused on the harvesting of mulberries and blackberries from plants on public and untended property.

During the summer, the Friends organize harvests in which members glean large yields of berries. These yields then form the basis for pies, jams and other berry-based goods created by the Friends. These goods are often exchanged for goods and services offering equivalent pleasures, both within and beyond the circle of the Friends, so that the circulation of berries functions to deepen and extend both friendships and community bonds.

*With few and fragile barriers to its occupation and use, unreal estate allows for secrets to be publicly exposed, accessible to all at the same time that they may be comprehensible to a few, or even to no one. Enigmatic graffiti, inscrutable signs, advertising campaigns that advertise only themselves: these are public secrets exposed on the underused and untended surfaces of unreal estate. It may also be the availability of these surfaces that inspire public secrecy—thoughts, expressions or forms that assume the status of a secret only with their public appearance.*

*While public secrets may be inscrutable even to their authors, their apparent mystery often prompts attempts at interpretation. Secrets can thereby be endowed with meanings, although what the disclosure of secrets usually bears are the desires, anxieties and dreams of those who attempt to decipher them.*

# Public Secrecy

# Hygienic Dress League

The Hygienic Dress League is a corporation that creates nothing but its own corporate image. It therefore uses videos, fashion shoots, branding and advertising not as means to the end of selling products or services but as reflexive artistic works. Recognizable as advertising, albeit of an enigmatic variety, these works invite questions about themselves (what exactly are they advertising?) and about corporate modes of identity and publicity more generally.

The League's project exploits the availability of urban space and urban surface in Detroit to *unprofitable expertise*. Its advertisements are painted on the boards that seal up abandoned buildings, re-purposing instruments of physical closure into ones of conceptual opening. Announcing the presence of the League and the "coming soon" of something left unspecified, these advertisements also focus attention on Detroit as an object of relentless campaigns of betterment. These campaigns, premised on the inadequacy or incompleteness of the city in its current state, pose Detroit's present as nothing but the pre-history of a hoped-for future. Exaggerating this condition, the Hygienic Dress League brings Detroit's obsessive futurology into public visibility and allows it to be newly scrutinized or resisted.

# Secret Pizza Party

Secret Pizza Party was a design studio founded and run by Josh Dunn and Andy DeGiulio, two graduates of Detroit's College of Creative Studies. As well as doing commercial work, the studio also engaged in ambient advertising campaigns in which signs were posted on the facades of abandoned buildings throughout Detroit. These signs depicted slogans that ran from the vaguely exhortative ("Make Things Better") to the enigmatically descriptive ("The Whole Why World").

The campaigns conducted by Secret Pizza Party exploited the surfaces of abandoned buildings as public space available for speech acts to a collective audience. These speech acts, though formatted like advertising, were conspicuously open-ended. "Make Things Better" seems an appropriate injunction to be made in Detroit, yet it does not describe *what* should be made better, *who* should make things better, and *how* things should be made better. "The Whole Why World" (from a 2006 *New York Times* article on second-graders, one of whom mistranslated the phrase "the whole wide world") similarly points to a city whose mysteries, challenges and problems continually provoke the question "why?" Both campaigns, then, alluded to Detroit's constantly narrated problems but left the identification and potential solutions to those problems unspecified and so up to its audience to determine.

Public Secrecy
## Trtl

In 2003 and 2004, abandoned buildings, bridges and road signs in and around downtown Detroit began to be tagged with graffiti featuring cartoon turtles and the words "trtl," "trdl," "turdl," "turtl," or "turtdlz." After turtles appeared on a sculpture outside of the Detroit Artists' Market and on the Detroit Institute of Art's regal building , turtle-tagging became the object of police attention, public critique and media speculation alike.

Most generally, turtles were understood to signify "slowness." Their status as subject matter for graffiti in Detroit was thus posed as a comment on the slowness with which Detroit was being reconstructed, as if the graffiti were calling for the eradication of the derelict surfaces on which they were themselves inscribed. More precisely, however, the enigmatic action of turtle-tagging converted the city's surfaces into mirrors that reflected the the city's own collective sense of itself. The "slowness" ascribed to the turtle-tagger, outed by the *Detroit Free Press* in 2004 as the graffiti artist, Ronald Scherz, was actually a product of the artist's audience. This audience saw an image they themselves projected onto turtles—the image of a city historically constructed on the basis of mobility and speed but one currently defined by torpor and inacitivity.

*Both within and beyond the city of unreal estate, the possibilities for sanctuary dwindle; there are fewer and fewer places offering haven or refuge. What replaces these places are facilities and centers—institutions where judgments are passed and fates decided. Sidewalks, parks and abandoned buildings house the homeless human remainder of this dynamic.*

*There are also places, however, where radical forms of hospitality continue to be extended. Sites of radical hospitality can extend no farther than a city block or encompass an entire neighborhood. They offer refuge both to the homeless and to those whose homes lose the capacity to shelter. These are places where visitors are welcomed as citizens of a usually disregarded or unknown city. This is the city of unreal estate—a city that shadows, faintly but fantastically, the city documented on maps, patrolled by authorities, divided into public and private, inhabited and empty, saved and lost.*

# Radical Hospitality

## Boggs Center

The Boggs Center was founded by friends and colleagues of Grace Lee Boggs and James Boggs, prominent community activists in Detroit, as a place to "honor and continue their legacy as movement activists and theoreticians." The Center is located at the Boggs home on the Eastside of Detroit. This location formalizes the status of that home as a community center and activist think tank, as well as exemplifies the unimportance of drawing firm boundaries between private and public space in the context of unreal estate.

The Center's positing of Detroit as a "city of hope" as opposed to a "city of despair" draws upon a conception of crisis as an opportunity to create new conditions of community, new forms of livelihood and new ways of thinking—a conception that also underlies the theory and practice of unreal estate. Among the many activities, programs and projects that take place at the Center are the Freedom Schooling Project, in which students, parents, teachers and community activists are brought together to discuss and create new models of education; the annual Detroit Summer, in which youth volunteers plant community gardens, paint public murals and participate in inter-generational dialogues with community elders; and the Detroit Asian Youth Project, in which Hmong and other Asian-American youth develop greater

awareness of identity, community and social justice issues. The staff at the Center also lead study groups, to learn from and about those involved in "transforming themselves and Detroit"; monthly conversations to "struggle around theory, vision and ideas, as well as ... ongoing practice"; and tours of Detroit that, in opposition to the prevalent blight tourism, focus on the city as site of activist labor and creative survival.

# Catherine Ferguson Academy

The Catherine Ferguson Academy is an alternative high school for pregnant young women and young mothers on the Westside of Detroit. Named after a freed slave who became an important promoter of education for impoverished children in New York City despite her illiteracy, the Academy allows its students to attend classes and care for their babies and young children in a single environment. Attending to both education and parenting, the Academy is a hybrid institution whose agenda has been transformed by the needs of its students.

As well as teaching a high-school curriculum, parenting, and college preparation skills, the Academy also makes prominent use of an urban farm. The farm is located on the site of property formerly used for high-school sports. The farm was initiated and is overseen by Paul Weertz, the Academy's science teacher, who also organized the farming
[p. 194] community on Farnsworth Street. Each student involved in the farm program tends her own plot in a vegetable or flower garden; students also work collectively in fruit orchards, beekeeping, and the raising of chickens, ducks, rabbits, goats and horses. Residents of Farnsworth Street, some of whom also teach at the Academy, raise feed for many of the farm's animals.

As well as reinforcing the teaching of parenting skills, work on the farm yields products such as goat milk, eggs, and honey, as well as fruit and vegetables, all used in the Academy's meal programs. But work on the farm also intersects with many other aspects of students' lives, from the reinforcement of familial traditions of gardening and cooking to the formation of new networks of friendship and community.

In the spring of 2011, as part of a large-scale corporatization of public services in Michigan, the Catherine Ferguson Academy and seven other Detroit-area schools were slated to be closed, along with the sale of 45 other Detroit-area schools to for-profit charter companies. Attempting to process unreal estate into real estate, this proposal represented a typical but wholly dysfunctional response to economic crisis.

# Block Clubbing

Block clubs exist throughout Detroit; they index the city's low level of municipal services and the corresponding need for city residents to provide those services themselves. They also reflect the high capacity for the self-organization of collective groups in a city where such organization is loosely supervised, if it is officially registered at all.

Block clubs often comprise organized systems to watch over neighborhoods where violence is frequent but police surveillance is low. As such, a large part of the block club's work is announcing its presence through signs and other visual media. Block clubs also [p.232] often function as collective agents of <u>blotting</u>; many vacant lots in neighborhoods with block clubs have been appropriated and used for such collective activities as gardening, barbequing or socializing. The accommodation of these activities by block clubs indicate how these clubs exceed any specific mandate they are formed to carry out and thereby enter into unreal estate speculation.

LCOME
TO
BULOUS
ENDER PL
REAT PLACE!

# Unsanctioned Collectives

**Temporary Communities
Do-It-Yourself-Then-Together
Micropolitanism
Urban Toeholds**

*The fragile and incomplete infrastructure of unreal estate supports
communities whose existence is also fragile and incomplete—temporary
communities that coalesce and disperse according to need, desire
or circumstance. A temporary community may emerge in response
to freedom or necessity; in either case, its location and duration
are provisional and often contingent on such imperatives as size of
membership, means of affiliation, accumulation of resources, or weather
conditions.*

*A straight bar might become queer for a night; a newly mown field might
become a gathering place for blues musicians and their audience; an
abandoned house might become a haunted house, inhabited by a circus
of lost souls. The limited duration of the temporary community allows it
to assume a flexible relationship to place and endows it with a nimble
ability to take advantage of unreal estate's low or non-existent barriers
to occupancy.*

# Temporary Communities

## Dally in the Alley

The Dally in the Alley is an annual community fair held in alleys, backyards and streets in the North Cass neighborhood in Detroit. The event began in 1977 as an inner-city art fair; it has subsequently evolved into a means to temporarily re-program disused and under-used urban space and to leverage that re-programming to support activist community initiatives. In its current form, the Dally includes a variety of recreational activities and events: musical performances, an art fair, and vendors selling crafts and food from tables and tents set up in streets and alleys.

Many of the initiatives supported by the Dally fill gaps left by Detroit's inadequate supply of municipal services: proceeds from the Dally have funded nighttime security in the North Cass neighborhood, a neighborhood soup kitchen, snow plowing in neighborhood alleys, trash pick-up, and the maintenance of a community garden. Other initiatives have been aimed against municipal policies and practices deemed harmful to the community. Most prominently, proceeds from the Dally have supported litigation against the Detroit Trash Incinerator, a waste disposal facility seen as a major cause of air pollution and pollution-related health problems in the city. The Dally thus comprises an adaptive reuse of urban space as a resource for the self-management of a community.

## Theatre Bizarre

Theatre Bizarre was a performance and party venue or "live-event playground" taking place on a complex of adjoining properties in the Highland Park neighborhood. It began when Ken Poiyer, owner of a house on W. State Fair Street and several adjacent vacant lots, offered space to his friend, the artist John Dunivant, for Dunivant's annual Halloween party. Dunivant had previously used the Russell Industrial Center for the party, building a shanty in the middle of the center and cutting scrub trees from city alleys to fashion a surreal Halloween environment. Poiyer's proposal enabled Dunivant to build a permanent and more extreme environment for the Halloween party, and then for other live theatre events, as well.

Dunivant conceived of the Theatre Bizarre Halloween party as an abandoned carnival that comes to life once a year in the mind of the fictional serial killer, Jacob Edward Torrent. Guests entered the party following the path that police had to take through Torrent's maze-like house, accessing the basement and then a tunnel Torrent dug out of a wall and up to the ground in his attempt to escape. Finally entering the party through a clown's mouth, guests were intended to feel as if they were inside Torrent's deranged consciousness, an experience that was amplified by costumes some guests worked on all year, as well as by

carnival exhibits like the Fiji Mermaid, Fortune Teller, Scaredy Cat Club and a homemade roller coaster.

As well as being used for public events like the Halloween party, the Stolen Media Festival, and the Squared Circle Review (a burlesque wrestling tournament), the Theatre Bizarre complex was also home to a group of tenants, a combination of Poiyer's family, friends and friends of friends. In 2009, Poiyer purchased two lots across an alley behind his complex, one empty and one with a salvageable house, as well as an adjacent house separated from his property by two burned and abandoned houses. This complex of owned and appropriated land would have enlarged Theatre Bizarre to the size of a city block. In the context of the Theatre, the block's decay would have become not a target of repair but an aesthetically evocative setting for unusual performances, parties and other events—a cultural resource to exploit and exaggerate. A week before the 2010 Halloween party, however, city officials shut down Theatre Bizarre, citing it for a number of code violations—one more instance of the city contributing to its own demise by failing to recognize the possibilities of unreal estate development.

# Detroit Guerrilla Queer Bar

The Detroit Guerrilla Queer Bar is a gay bar that roams through Detroit, each month swarming an existing straight bar for one evening. Members of the group are informed online of the location of the Guerrilla Queer Bar in the days before a swarm is to take place; the bar and its patrons are left uninformed. The result is, initially, confusion, especially when, according the group's director, "we colonize bars that attract a crowd that is the diametric opposite of ours." After confusion, however, comes the emergence of unusual circumstances in which unprecedented kinds of social interaction can develop, with otherwise-separated individuals and communities mingling in close proximity.

The Guerrilla Queer Bar does not formalize a space for a gay bar. Instead, the dislocation of its members becomes the point of departure for an inventive spatial practice that yields both temporary spaces and temporary communities, each of whose nature is unpredictable and variable. The Guerrilla Queer Bar's disinterest in transforming real estate precisely maps onto its traffic with unreal estate—alternative forms of urban inhabitation. "Part of the fun is not knowing who's who or what's going on": this evocation of a Guerrilla Queer Bar party eloquently registers the type of possibilities that unreal estate opens up.

# John's Carpet House

In the mid 1980s, John Estes built a shed next to his house on the Eastside of Detroit, lined the shed with carpets for sound insulation, and founded an urban juke joint where local blues musicians played during spring, summer and early fall Sunday afternoons. Estes was both a scrapper and a blues musician; what became known as John's Carpet House was based on both of Estes' skills, as well as on the possibility to translate a rural form of public space to Detroit's depleted urban landscape.

After Estes died in 2006, his friend, Pete Barrow, took over John's Carpet House. Several years later, a fire burned down the Carpet House along with Estes' house next door—an event that was far from atypical in the neighborhood. Barrow then moved the Sunday blues performances to the vacant lot across the street, formerly occupied by the Carpet House's audience. On Sundays, Barrow brings a portable generator, mows grass, lays down a single plane of carpet to define a stage, and organizes and deejays performances. The audience of these performances supplies its own chairs and sometimes tables, coolers and barbeques, producing a participatory outdoor juke joint.

# Tashmoo Biergarten

The Tashmoo Biergarten is a pop-up beer garden located on three vacant lots in Detroit's West Village. The lots are owned by a non-profit development company; while they remain undeveloped, a consortium of local residents initiated the beer garden as an interim use that could nimbly convert open space into an urban amenity.

Place and time are consumed along with beer, sausages and pretzels at the beer garden. The beer garden serves up an experience of "locality" by offering beer from Michigan breweries, snacks from local food vendors, and benches and tables constructed of lumber reclaimed from Detroit's demolished buildings. It similarly serves up an experience of "history"; the name "Tashmoo" refers to a Native American word for "meeting place," an amusement park built in the late 19th century on an island in Lake St. Claire, and a famous steamboat that plied Lake St. Claire in the first decades of the 20th century. A house owned by a member of the Tashmoo's crew, demolished in 2011, stood on one of the lots on which the beer garden takes place, thus pinning place and time together.

The community that forms at the beer garden is allied by more or less intense affiliations to the place and time consolidated by the project, but also by more or less intense desires for *somewhere* and *sometime*—longings for spatial and temporal location. The beer garden allows these longings to be symbolically sated, satisfied without a commitment to any particular place and time—satisfied, in other words, by unreal means.

*To do it yourself, rather than to rely on others to do it, is to reclaim responsibility for creating what you need and want, and to even open the possibility of needing or wanting something novel or different. In some form, the do-it-yourselfer is a contemporary changeling, a passive consumer transmuted into an active producer. But this consumer and this producer are solitary, working alone, fitting neatly into the free market's society of disagreggated individuals—a society where the urgency of solidarity is directly proportional to the experience of oppression.*

*There are also places, however, where doing it collectively becomes desirable—where collaborative forms of work and play hover in between exercises of freedom and imperatives of survival. These places occupy unreal estate—property where knowledge, skill and imagination can be exchanged in lieu of money. To collectivize do-it-yourself culture is to transform that culture from an assemblage of individuals to a community of shared interests and blurry relations. These communities are intimate; to do-it-yourself-then-together is to fabricate or rely upon relations of trust, affection, familiarity or solidarity.*

# Do-It-Yourself-Then-Together

Do-It-Yourself-Then-Together

# UFO Factory

The UFO Factory was a self-described "art/design and sound production company, recording studio, art gallery, nite klub, etc..." The three members of the UFO Factory, Davin Brainard, Dion Fischer and Warn Defever, originally met in the late 1990s at Zoot's Coffee House, in the Cass Corridor. Zoot's was itself an unreal estate site—a self-avowed social experiment as much as a business, it provided a place for the Cass Corridor's diverse communities of musicians, artists, poets, freeks and others to meet, mingle and perform experimental music. The UFO Factory, housed in a warehouse near Detroit's produce market, Eastern Market, furthered such interaction; the UFO Factory provided a venue for both art exhibitions and live music performances, especially by musicians who had played at Zoot's, Detroit Art Space and other spaces that hosted innovative music.

Members of the UFO Factory were part of some of the noise bands that performed at the Factory, such as Princess Dragonmom, His Name is Alive and Metal Dungeon; they also released noise and experimental music through the Time Stereo label and organized the annual "Noise Camp," a festival of noise and experimental music hosted at the [p.268] Contemporary Art Institute of Detroit. Some of the art work displayed in exhibitions at the UFO Factory emerged from an intersection of art

and music, including cover art and packaging for cassette tapes, LPs and CDs; posters for concerts; etchings into vinyl; and fanzines that made music when played on a turntable.

The UFO Factory exemplified the capacity of unreal estate to support non-commercial art and music. More importantly, however, it also displayed the ability of unreal estate to blur the boundary between audience, performer and artist and to thereby form new communities of interest in which the do-it-yourself ethic of experimental art and music was extended and collectivized.

Do-It-Yourself-Then-Together
## Yes Farm

The Yes Farm is an artists' collective in which "art" encompasses a
wide range of practices, from the cultivation of community gardens,
through the staging of performances with neighborhood children,
to the curation of music and dance concerts and open-submission
art exhibitions. In the context of these practices, "life" is not a mere
support structure for "art," but is, rather, a field which is shaped by
art's aesthetic and ideological values.

The work of the Yes Farm takes place in a neighborhood that is also a
[p.194] focus of the farming community on <u>Farnsworth Street</u>. "The arts pay
an important role in the community," according to the Yes Farm, which
thereby seeks "to bring art into the lives of the people and places
around us." This belief and goal are distinguished by the small scale
of the community that the Yes Farm attempts to foster: a community
centered on and around the unique block where the Yes Farm
is located.

In the frame of the Yes Farm's *intimate community*, the dynamics that
are valued in the free market economy—publicity, accumulation,
development and, most especially, growth—are thrown into question.
Eschewing both these values and the systems from which these values

emerge, the Yes Farm's relationship to its social context is subtly but decisively different from other community-based art practices in Detroit. The Yes Farm is not a community-building project that regards an existing community as somehow flawed or inadequate and that invokes some other, seemingly superior community-yet-to-come. Instead, it positions itself in an existing community and seeks to find opportunities and possibilities to work within that community on its own terms. This project is based on a radical acceptance of existing conditions and a radical suspension of programs to "improve" the lives of others, whether by art or any other means.

The city of unreal estate is punctuated by havens, pockets, isolated islands, narrow interstices. These are the micropolitan worlds of intentional or impulsive collectives: urban farmers clustered on a city block, a subculture thriving at the tail of a dead-ended street, a complex of houses sheltering immigrants from the city of real estate.

Are other worlds possible? The wish for such worlds is insistent, but evidence of them is fugitive. A micropolitan enclave is a place that might also comprise a world, a world worth wanting at a downsized scale. The inhabitation of these worlds is not at all revolutionary; the micropolitan enclave offers a place not to wait for revolution, or even want revolution, but to withdraw from that particular state of affairs that passes for objective reality: to refuse, to differ, to disappear, to live otherwise.

# Micropolitanism

Micropolitanism
# Farnsworth Street

p.150] In the mid 1980s, Paul Weertz, a science teacher at the <u>Catherine Ferguson Academy</u>, bought a number of houses on a single block of Farnsworth Street, on Detroit's depopulated and decaying Eastside. Weertz renovated one house for his family and rented out other houses on the block. He also began to farm vacant land on and around the block, on both property that he owned and property that he appropriated. Over time, other people involved in urban farming have moved to his block on Farnsworth Street, including collectives like p.188] the <u>Yes Farm</u>. The block is currently the site of a number of gardens, an orchard, and a population of people who farm around the area—a micropolitan urban enclave. These farms yield alfalfa and hay, fruit and vegetables, honey, eggs and goat's milk, among other products. The alfalfa and hay are used to feed animals at the <u>Catherine Ferguson Academy</u>, where a number of the blocks' residents work, while other farm products are consumed by the farmers and their community.

The development of an urban farming community on Farnsworth Street would be impossible without the availability of unreal estate on and around that street, not only for farming but also for the accommodation of farmers in close proximity. But few, if any, of these farmers are *only* farmers; Farnsworth Street is a *grassroots*

*live-work-play* community whose diverse members exchange skills and interests and are thus able to participate in hybridized forms of cross-activism, with guerilla farmers, artists, musicians and bicycle repairers often merging projects and involvements.

Micropolitanism
# Fourth Street

In the 1950s, the construction of the campus of Wayne State University and then Interstate Highway 94 destroyed most of Fourth Street, a long street running north and south on Detroit's Westside. A tiny one-block-long section of the street was preserved, however, isolated just behind Highway 94. In the 1960s, this block became a haven for artists, musicians and activists, many of whom were involved in the Cass Corridor counterculture. The block has remained an *intentional urban community* that occupies a small but complex structure of public and private spaces.

On Fourth Street, these spaces are tightly enmeshed with one another, so that both "private spaces" like front porches and "public spaces" like vacant lots function as living and dining rooms for the street's residents. Vacant lots on and around the street have thus become spaces for community gardens, fire circle, picnic table, volleyball court, chess games and dog park. The residents of Fourth Street also host an annual street fair that celebrates Detroit culture through the participation of local musicians, local artists and local producers of food and merchandise.

The isolation and fragmentation of Fourth Street are crucial to the community that has developed and evolved on the street; the physical separation of Fourth Street from its urban context has allowed its residents to organize themselves and their environment. The Fourth Street community, then, is able to support values, ideals and practices that diverge from the communities around it.

# Trumbullplex

Trumbullplex is an anarchist-oriented collective house and performance and exhibition space. Its original five members purchased a complex of two houses and studio space that had a long history in Detroit's artistic counterculture. The sculptor and painter, Arthur Wenk, member of the activist artists' collective, Common Ground, purchased the complex in the late 1960s, converting what was an armory into an artist studio and occupying a floor of one of the houses. In the late 1970s, the complex was bought and sold several times, the last time to theatre director, Peter Malette. Malette had a stage and sound booth built in the former studio space, which he then used for community theatre productions. Malette, in turn, sold the property to an anarchist group in 1993 for the almost symbolic price of $2,500.

The members of Trumbullplex share in household duties, make all decisions and agendas on the basis of consensus agreement, and practice an *impulsive collectivity* in which group activities are less enforced than improvised. Trumbullplex also hosts a variety of activities that critically engage with Detroit, with its public space providing a venue for art exhibitions, concerts, film screenings and theatre performances, each funded only by voluntary donations. In addition, Trumbullplex houses the Idle Kids Zine Library, an extensive

collection of zines and activist literature that was compiled at the now-closed Idle Kids Books and Records Shop in the Cass Corridor. Members of Trumbullplex cultivate community gardens both on their own property and on adjacent appropriated property; many members are also involved in the <u>Earthworks Urban Farm</u>, the <u>Catherine Ferguson Academy</u> and other urban agriculture ventures, as well as The Hub, a Cass Corridor cycling non-profit.

[p.40]
[p.150]

The contributions that members of Trumbullplex make to the city, both individually and collectively, are enabled and intensified by the physical location of the group on unreal estate—a site whose occupation is not economically constrained and so one that allows the attention and energy of its occupants to be directed outwards, with precise intentionality and heightened effect.

LISTENER

DIY PLAY

OLD TIME MUSIC
Pedal Shop

BASEMENT UNICORN
SHADOW PUPPET SHOW

WHY I A
BE CAR

TERRA
ZOA

CARA G. IMP

AT THE

Trumbu

FRIDAY
JULY 31

Night Owl
+
Jeffrey William Thomas
(Tape release!) +
BEE
KEEPERS!
AT:
TRUMBULL
PLEX
THEATRE

4210 TRUMBULL ST. DETROIT, MI

*To relinquish the thought that the city is already understood is to open the city to curiosity, scrutiny, description and interpretation. The city becomes enigmatic, uninhabited by received ideas and uncultivated by conventional thought. The urban wilderness—a typical figure for the city of unreal estate—can be investigated from a station. This station is a neighborhood outpost, a toehold on the quotidian of others, a residency for those wishing to learn more about the city.*

*What can a stranger know? Temporary resident of an urban toehold, a stranger can never know what residents of the neighborhood around that toehold know. The knowledge assimilated while in residence at the toehold, however, is not less than local knowledge as much as different than this knowledge: another apprehension of the city, with its own particular uses and values.*

# Urban Toeholds

# Center for Creative eXchange

The Center for Creative eXchange was envisioned by its founder,
Phaedra Robinson, as a conduit for "creative energy" to flow into and
out of Detroit. The physical location of the center was a burned-out
house in the Woodbridge neighborhood, purchased by Robinson from
the City of Detroit. The house was to serve as a venue for exhibitions
and performances, community gardening and recycling, and
residencies for artists and writers. These activities were to develop
synergistically: gardens would provide food to nourish resident
artists and writers; these artists and writers would create exhibitions
and performances and/or assist in the rehabilitation of the center's
building; visitors to the center would sponsor work by its resident
artists and writers, and so on. During the reconstruction of the physical
space in which it was housed, the center also sponsored events such
as a "Gallery Bike Crawl," in which visitors rode a route connecting art
studios and galleries in and near downtown Detroit.

While the programs envisioned by the center were to function
synergistically, these programs also comprised an assemblage of *post-industrial urban therapies,* each seeking to re-vision the possibilities
inherent in Detroit's conditions of disinvestment and depopulation.
This re-visioning framed Detroit not as a crisis or disaster, but as a

context for new kinds of creative production and exchange. In 2009, the building that housed the center was put up for sale; this building then re-entered Detroit's landscape of empty houses and became available for other uses, licit or illicit, reactionary or progressive, therapeutic or dangerous.

Urban Toeholds
# Filter Detroit

Filter Detroit is a guest residence for artists and researchers sited
[p.246] in a house in North Hamtramck, across the street from the <u>Power</u>
[p.242] <u>House</u> and blocks away from the <u>Full Scale Design Lab</u>. The project was
initiated by Kerstin Niemann, a Hamburg-based curator who, as a guest
curator with the Van Abbe Museum in Eindhoven, the Netherlands,
worked on the "Heartland" exhibition about innovative artistic
production in the American Midwest. Filter Detroit is an attempt
to further this production by providing a place for information and
inspiration to be exchanged between "artists, visionaries and thinkers
from the region as well as the outside." It is also at attempt to direct
creative thought specifically toward urban initiatives, with Detroit
considered as both a place of challenge and opportunity.

As well as providing a physical site for exchange to take place, Filter
Detroit intends to comprise a "living archive" where knowledge about
alternative urban initiatives in Detroit is deposited and consolidated.
As such, the project intends to institutionalize a process that otherwise
occurs in a more-or-less unplanned and decentralized manner.

Urban Toeholds
# Ego Circus

Ego Circus is an invitation-only residency for artists and architects in Hamtramck. The residency is sited in a house purchased in 2008 by an anonymous group of recent graduates of the Cranbrook Academy of Art. Unlike perhaps every other residency program in Detroit, Ego Circus explicitly extricates itself from the businesses of "saving the neighborhood," "building the community," or providing another sort of social service through art and architecture. Rather, Ego Circus informs its residents that they are free to experiment in their medium without fulfilling any putative social function—a freedom that is permitted, according to Ego Circus, by the vast oversupply of houses in the depopulated city of Detroit.

The stated backgrounding of art and architecture as social practices of course renders the precise social status of art and architecture as fraught—far more fraught than when there is a tacit agreement on the social valence of these disciplines. The freedom to experiment in and on the house where Ego Circus is based has thus yielded a series of anxious meditations on the ambitions, achievements and evaluative criteria of artistic and architectural research.

These meditations have almost all taken the form of site-specific interventions in the Ego Circus house, interventions that become mere raw material for alteration when a subsequent cohort of residents arrive. The work that Ego Circus fosters, then, leaves no lasting trace, except in photographic documentation; autonomous artistic and architectural research is performed on the remains of autonomous artistic and architectural research. "No-one was harmed in the making of this work," Ego Circus announces at its exhibitions—but this is a claim that could also be understood to poignantly contradict its intention to liberate art and architecture from social responsibility.

# Unsolicited Constructions

**Accidental Architecture**
**Extreme Housework**
**Scavenged Space**
**Patrimony of the Unlost**

*If architecture is, among other things, an ensemble of concepts and practices that regulate the fabrication of buildings, then architecture could be bracketed before buildings are constructed or reconstructed. This bracketing might comprise a metropolitan form of "architecture without architects"—a kind of building usually discovered on the fringes of global modernity.*

*Modernity, however, is fringed both from within and without; it is fissured, hollowed out in places, riven by gaps. Its uneven distribution creates situations where architecture can be left behind, leaving merely space, volume and ground in its place. The juxtapositions and intersections that ensue are incongruous and gorgeous, violent and absurd. To discover these architectural accidents is to recognize the sublime force of circumstance: the innovation that happens when the attempt to make something happen is surrendered or ignored.*

# Accidental Architecture

# Michigan Building Parking Garage

The Michigan Building was opened in 1925 in downtown Detroit. It originally contained a block of offices and the "French Renaissance" style Michigan Theatre. The Michigan Theatre contained a large auditorium with over 4,000 seats, an intricately detailed proscenium, mezzanine, roof, balconies and lobby, and stage with Wurlitzer organ and orchestra pit. In the 1950s, 60s and 70s, as a result of declining audiences and the more general decline of downtown Detroit, the theater was transformed into a movie palace, pornographic film venue, supper club and rock concert venue; none of these ventures proved profitable and the last of several interim closures took place in 1976. At the same time, tenants in the office block adjacent to the theater demanded "secure parking" from the owners of the Michigan Building. The owners proposed to demolish the unused theater and replace it with a parking garage; due to structural conditions, however, the theater could not be demolished without threatening the adjacent office block. A solution was then improvised; a three level steel and concrete parking structure was inserted into the theater's empty shell, leaving much of the theater's original architecture intact.

The inadvertent result of the transformation of the theater into a parking garage is a space of enormous aesthetic effect and historical resonance. This effect and resonance emerged not because the theater was valued as a work of architecture or historic monument, but precisely because it was *not* valued as such. For the owners of the Michigan Building, the theater comprised merely valueless empty space; this perception of emptiness yielded an act of *accidental preservation* whose formal and historical properties diverge from, and perhaps exceed, any deliberately conceived work of heritage conservation.

# Peacemakers International

Peacemakers International is a Christian ministry located in a group
of buildings in a disadvantaged neighborhood on Detroit's Eastside.
For Peacemakers, this neighborhood provides a field of opportunity
to engage with the "many precious souls who lie in this vast inner city
wasteland, waiting to be rescued by the blood of Jesus Christ and
rescued from Satan's capacity." Poverty, that is, provides conditions to
Peacemakers that are particularly conducive to missionary work—the
loss of economic value of property in its neighborhood produces the
possibility to cultivate otherwise-inaccessible spiritual values.

The community activities of Peacemakers include church services,
prayer meetings, a soup kitchen open for breakfast and lunch three
times a week, and the hosting of activities for neighborhood children.
Members of the Peacemakers ministry live and work in several adjacent
buildings. Much of the work of these members is focused on urban
agriculture, with gardens both inside and around abandoned buildings
providing produce for the soup kitchen and sale to a commercial
vendor, as well. The ministry's gardens inside a roofless and otherwise
empty building comprise a remarkable example of unreal estate; the
gardens are made possible by the evacuation of all architectural value
from the building and the subsequent emergence of the building's
footprint as its only resource for development.

# Blotting

The many vacant lots in Detroit allow both new sorts of public uses and new forms of private dwelling. One form of the latter takes place when homeowners appropriate, borrow or purchase vacant lots adjacent to their property and expand that property to a new, larger size. This expansion produces what the design studio, Interboro Partners, has termed "blots"—a hybrid urban space that functions as both a "block" and a "lot."

Blotting emerged as a grassroots form of residential property development. Since the early 2000s, however, the City of Detroit has officially sponsored blotting by selling vacant lots under city ownership to adjacent homeowners or other neighborhood residents for nominal prices ($150 to $500) and by allowing vacant lots to be used for gardens under the Adopt-A-Lot program. This sponsorship reflects the municipal utility of blotting as an occupation of otherwise abandoned urban space.

Blots have been used by homeowners in a variety of ways, from parking cars, through gardening, to simply enlarging front or back yards. While these uses are not at all radical in themselves, the process by which

these uses take place is specific to cities of unreal estate like Detroit. In these cities, the creation of blots transforms empty space that is valueless to its formal owner (typically the city, county or state) to space endowed with new values by new users or owners.

Where there is a surplus of houses, the house is available for extreme housework. This work takes the house as something that can be taken apart—carved up, tricked out, faked, parodied, re-assembled or given over to hitherto undomesticated needs and desires. Extreme housework is dedicated, then, not to house cleaning or home maintenance but to passionately rendering the house anew.

In the city of unreal estate, there is a great deal of this housework left to be done, but there is also a great deal of time in which to do this work. No one waits for extreme housework to be completed so that no one is bothered by its deferral. Abandoned houses spread slowly across the city's depleted terrain. Once in a while, extreme housework will transform one of these houses into something else, but something that satisfies no need for comfort or shelter. The need is for something different: what estranges the days, what beguiles the city, what renders architecture unfamiliar to itself.

# Extreme Housework

Extreme Housework
# Detroit Industrial Gallery

[p.286] The Detroit Industrial Gallery is a house/urban art work in the midst of the Heidelberg Project. Its creator, the artist Tim Burke, purchased a piece of property on the Heidelberg Project's block and then re-purposed an existing house as a work of art. Greatly indebted to the Heidelberg Project, Burke collects and exhibits abandoned objects on and around his house's walls and grounds.

The aesthetic effect of the Detroit Industrial Gallery is far less vivid than that of the Heidelberg Project—it is at once derivative of its precedent but also devoid of that precedent's discomforting conjoining of mourning and celebration. Yet the Detroit Industrial Gallery was endowed with entirely new levels of meaning and import when, in the spring of 2009, Burke introduced the project to the market economy by placing a "For Sale" sign on his front door. The sign announced an asking price of $1,000,000,000 dollars; simultaneously, Burke listed the Detroit Industrial Gallery on eBay, asking for a starting bid of $500,000 dollars.

Describing his thoughts on putting his house up for sale, Burke wrote in his blog, "Why not stimulate the Detroit real estate market? Let's get things moving in Detroit again!" Thus, precisely the imperatives of the

market economy that many artists of urban renewal explicitly attempt to refuse ("we're not in this to make any money...") became the objects of Burke's engagement. This engagement, however, was an overt over-identification in which the market was neither an object of denial nor an instrument of exploitation, but rather a site of play. For sale, whether for $500,000 or $1,000,000,000, the Detroit Industrial Gallery was endowed with a value that was wholly unreal—an endowment that, in turn, raised questions about the reality of values that the market economy so routinely fabricates.

Extreme Housework
# Full Scale Design Lab

[p.246] Occupying a fire-damaged North Hamtramck house owned by Power House co-owner, Mitch Cope, the Full Scale Design Lab was a platform for experimental architectural alterations. The members of the Lab were fellows in the Architecture Program at the University of Michigan. Taking advantage of the house's position outside the market economy, the Lab apprehended the house as site on which to conduct "full scale" architectural experiments that would be precluded anywhere architecture possessed value as real estate.

The experiments were formal interventions that were tied to loosely defined or experiential programs. One intervention took the form of a movable room that could be pushed outside the house, where it would offer entry to the house; another illuminated the house's windowless garage with one thousand glass tubes inserted into the garage's wood-frame walls; still another created a new wedge-shaped room, with bleacher seating and a skylight, within the house's existing volume.

Approaching the house primarily as form, the work of the Lab extended a venerable tradition of architectural thinking and making. This tradition has been focused on the disciplinary and professional possibilities of architecture. Detroit's unreal estate offers a plenitude

of sites where such possibilities can be explored. At the same time, the concept of unreal estate also discloses the horizons of thinking about architecture as a discipline or profession; architecture in the city of unreal estate is often authored without architects, on the basis of forms of knowledge exterior and irrelevant to architecture-as-such.

## Power House

The Power House is a self-styled "social art project" taking form through the renovation of a damaged house in North Hamtramck. Conducted by Mitch Cope and Gina Reichert, who together comprise the art/design group, Design 99, the renovation is intended to yield not only a model home but also a site of neighborhood interaction, a catalyst for new ideas about community-building, and a stimulus for new social networks. Based on these intentions, Cope and Reichert pose their interventions at the Power House as components of a "crude performance," a process at once artistic, architectural and social, that is the fundamental work of the project.

The focus on the process of the Power House's renovation, rather than on the product that is the outcome of this process, gives the project a unique architectural temporality. While speed is valued in market-based renovations, slowness is valued at the Power House; *slow building* allows each intervention to be considered on its own terms, resourced by unique or found materials, and carried out with attention to its performative dimension.

As one of the most widely known urban art projects in Detroit, the Power House has also consolidated an audience far beyond its

immediate neighborhood, an effect perhaps unanticipated but one that has introduced a highly-salient dimension to the project's performative status. Serving as a reference for many different ideas of artistic agency in post-industrial Detroit, the Power House has become a kind of icon of unreal estate, a figure for an entire range of creative possibilities emerging from Detroit's decline. The Power House project has also come to include the support of other projects that animate vacant homes by various sorts of artistic or cultural ambitions; these projects, [p.212] all in the Power House's neighborhood, include <u>Filter Detroit</u> and the [p.242] <u>Full Scale Design Lab</u>.

*The city of unreal estate is a city of apparent vacancy, emptiness and abandonment. And yet, to a gaze that sees not much left, what's left over assumes new significance. Remnants, traces, bits and pieces, odds and ends: all these can assume a newly vivid materiality and accommodate a newly expanded set of use values.*

*Some of this leftover detritus is spatial. Down an alley, in a garage, parties are thrown on spring and summer evenings; in a vacant lot, a crowd gathers to watch a performance; in a former union hall, in a city with less and less unionized work, music is made and played. Spaces empty out, lie abandoned, and are then re-discovered. These re-discoveries may in turn be discovered as scavengers of events, pastimes, and entertainments come across them.*

# Scavenged Space

Scavenged Space
# Alley Culture

Alley Culture is a gallery in a converted garage behind a house in the Woodbridge neighborhood of Detroit. The gallery displays works by contemporary artists on exposed wood-frame walls, with visitors kept warm in the winter by a wood-burning stove. The hidden urban setting and unfinished architectural form of Alley Culture correspond to the gallery's alternative curatorial program, described by its founders as "a cross-pollination of politics, geography and generations." This cross-pollination is made manifest in Alley Culture's hybrid status as both an exhibition space and a community meeting place. "The Art World is not to be differentiated from the Hood": this claim, set out on the gallery's website, is central to both Alley Culture's location and work.

One of the founders of Alley Culture, the artist Sherry Hendrick, was a member of a Manhattan-based art group Collaborative Projects (Colab), which was dedicated to collaboration both between the members of the group and between the group and the public. During its lifetime in the 1980s, Collaborative Projects organized many of Manhattan's politically progressive artists and exploited the availability of under-used or unused property in the city.

Alley Culture translates the ambitions of Collaborative Projects
to Detroit and to Detroit's specific conditions, challenges and
possibilities. As well as hosting curated exhibitions, Alley Culture also
organizes "Voice of the People" exhibitions, determined by artists
who choose to participate in them; annual seed exchanges, where
locally grown organic seeds are distributed; occasional showings of
alternative films; and a web-based listing of local shops and services.
This complex mix of activities is focused by the gallery's interest
in sustaining neighborhood and urban culture and resisting the
homogenizing forces of conventional urban "development."

Scavenged Space
# Grafikjam Alleys

The Grafikjam Alleys are a series of alleys in a section of Southwest
Detroit where home owners have allowed their garages to be graffitied
by neighborhood youth. These youth were brought into an urban art
program, "Grafikjam," by the neighborhood organization, Young Nation.
In this program, urban art, and, in particular, graffiti, is used as an
entry-point into a pedagogy of drawing, painting and "community
responsibility"—an obligation to maintain the quality of life in a
neighborhood. Program participants are given material to paint
garages; they are also conscripted to remove "non-permissive graffiti"
on other buildings in the neighborhood.

The division of graffiti into "permitted" and "non-permitted" forms, the
division of buildings into acceptable and unacceptable sites for graffiti,
and the top-down formation of a socially responsible graffiti crew
represent attempts to simultaneously encourage and domesticate
personal expression. At the same time, however, the Grafikjam Alleys
supercede the limits of the program that produced them; it is not only
the product of an attempt to corral graffiti into socially acceptable
forms, practices and spaces, but also a novel transformation of
one part of the single-family home into a publicly available site of
expressive creativity.

Scavenged Space
# The Lot

The Lot was an outdoor exhibition venue founded by Kathy Leisen. Originally located in North Corktown, next door to Leisen's house, The Lot consisted of two empty house plots. According to Leisen, exhibitions in this space were "designed to challenge the way we think about the context of art, community, and dialogue by highlighting the value and joy of experimentation." This mission was accomplished by opening The Lot to "a diversity of local, national, and international artists, both emerging and established artists, writers, waitresses, taxi drivers, hair stylists, athletes, office assistants, historians, dental hygienists, and pop singers"— in another words, to a range of communities, whether existing, possible or imagined. If The Lot was a community-building project, then this building was not a reconstruction of an already-extant community identified with the already-extant topography of a neighborhood. Rather, "community" was here an object to investigate, re-think and design, as well as something that could transcend its customary "local" limits.

The conversion of crab grass covered vacant lots into a venue for art was accomplished by almost no physical transformation of the site; only freestanding letters spelling "The Lot" identified the site. After two years, The Lot became a nomadic exhibition venue, temporarily

occupying other vacant lots in Detroit, again identified only by freestanding letters. The Lot's spatialization, then, was primarily conceptual, based on an understanding of vacancy not as a problem to fix but an opportunity to exploit; "site-specificity" here became an appreciation of what is absent from a site, as well as what is present.

## Submerge

Submerge is the major production and distribution company for electronic music in Detroit. For Mike Banks, the company's co-founder, this music possesses vital cultural and political agencies in the post-industrial city—a place where predominantly African-American populations are "bombarded by audio and visual stereotypes that are essentially a guide for failure." Banks thereby creates and curates music as part of an "ongoing Electronic Warfare with the programmers who seek to contain our minds."

Detroit techno—the city's particular version of electronic music—is not only characterized by its layered sound, fast tempo, and engagement with funk music, but also by its mode of production. Many early techno musicians chose to found their own independent labels, giving them ownership and control of their work, but also many administrative challenges. In the late 1980s, Submerge was co-founded by Banks, then part of the music collective, Underground Resistance, and Christa Weatherspoon; it was intended as a platform to support independent music collectives in Detroit, allowing them to share business services and know-how so that they could distribute their work most effectively.

In 2002, Submerge completed the renovation of a former laundry workers union hall into a new building to replace its former "appointment-only" headquarters. This new building includes a series of venues to complement those of the club, where the public most often encounters dance music: "Exhibit: 3000," a museum dedicated to preserving the history of Detroit electronic music; "Somewhere in Detroit," a record store and meeting place for electronic music listeners; and the "Metroplex Room," a space for film screenings, exhibitions, discussions, seminars and parties.

With its variety of spaces and programs, the Submerge building allows music to not only be produced and consumed, but also imagined, experienced, archived, studied and discussed—each an activity that is capable of releasing music's activist force. According to Banks, "by using the untapped energy potential of sound we are going to destroy this wall (between races) in much the same way as certain frequencies shatter glass"; unreal estate makes urban space available for this, and other, counter-hegemonic projects.

THERE'S NO LOVE
LIKE DETROIT
LOVE!
LOOK AROUND
"SKURGE"

2 MY Xtended fam
IN DETROIT THANKS 4 EVERYTHING
You guyz really made a difference
in my life thanx u all the
x support + love!

There's No Love Like Detroit Love!

Come
on
Insomnia
Ball Grill
with
Tokyo
sibuya

LOSER

UR
Very

N.Y Techno = www.gothamgrooves.com

ありがとう
Let us in
yoko  contact-Records.com

PARIS
WAS HERE

LAHAYA

Lance Holland

peace
from
Clove

SUBMERGE
3000 - 310

18 DEE

I Love D

高橋勇次参上!

日本代表

# Contemporary Art Institute of Detroit

The Contemporary Art Institute of Detroit was founded in 1979 by
Detroit-based artists Charles McGee and Jean Hielbrunn. Its founding
was a response to Detroit's condition as a place where contemporary
art was intensively produced, but also where public venues for
exhibiting this art were lacking. While the institutionalization
of art often implies a stifling of creativity, initiative and vision,
the Contemporary Art Institute of Detroit assayed a *critical
institutionalization,* a deployment of institutionality against the grain by
a self-organized artists' collective dedicated to the production of new
connections between art and community.

For its first twenty-five years of existence, the Institute functioned
nomadically, organizing and curating exhibitions and installations at
a series of public sites throughout Detroit. In 2004, the Institute took
over a building that was occupied by Detroit Contemporary, a gallery
in operation from 1998 to 2003 that was co-founded by artists Aaron
[p.208] Timlin and Phaedra Robinson, founder of the Center for Creative
eXchange.

The Detroit Contemporary building, owned by Timlin, was a formerly abandoned house sited amidst many vacant lots in the Woodbridge neighborhood. Located in this building, the Institute has been able to greatly broaden its activities, curating not only a regular series of art exhibitions but also a variety of music, dance, and other performance-based events, many of them organized by community groups. At the same time, the location of the Institute in a fraught urban site where "art," contemporary or otherwise, appears to be fugitive or absent has only heightened the tendentious nature of the Institute's own institutionality.

With their caretakers frequently preoccupied with immediate tasks of survival, objects in the city of unreal estate are often left behind, disowned or abandoned. Precisely as such, however, these objects offer themselves for repossession, for becoming strange in new hands.

Yet it's not only objects that are lost in the city of unreal estate, but also identities, ambitions and plans of action; the city alienates both objects from subjects and subjects from themselves. Thus, the finders of lost objects can also, as it is said, "find themselves." Accumulating and arranging castoffs and discards, they become caretakers, curators, or outsider artists, claiming unreal estate to archive and arrange unreal estate's particular material culture.

# Patrimony of the Unlost

# Hamtramck Disneyland

In 1990, a Ukranian emigrant and retired General Motors autoworker named Dmytro Szylak began to scavenge abandoned objects from the streets of Hamtramck and to assemble those objects on and around two garages he owned. The objects he assembled were the detritus of middle-class American popular culture: bicycle wheels, toy dolls, pots of artificial flowers, model airplanes, Christmas lights, Elvis paintings, wooden soldiers, flags and signs. Reversing the regimented labor of the Fordist assembly line, Szylak's assemblage is ad hoc, unplanned and accretive; pieces are added, one by one, to a work that is constantly in flux.

Amid criticism from his neighbors in the early 1990s, Szylak's self-titled "Ukraine and Amerika Disneyland" was termed "art" by the then-mayor of Hamtramck, who himself studied sculpture at the nearby Cranbrook Academy of Fine Art. As a work of art, the project was protected by the City of Hamtramck from demolition. In the years since, what has become known as Hamtramck Disneyland has continued to grow and develop.

[p.286] Unlike Detroit's best-known example of an urban found-art environment, Tyree Guyton's <u>Heidelberg Project,</u> Hamtramck Disneyland is not posed by its author as a means of "healing communities through art." Indeed, Hamtramck Disneyland is not scripted as anything except "art"; it is only described by a sign that reads "Welcome to Art Show" and copies of newspaper articles about the project that are displayed, under transparent plastic, amid the project's many other bits and pieces. The project's intentions and meanings are left undefined, and thus, left to its audience to decipher, or not.

## Car Wash Café

The Car Wash Café was an open-air auto storage facility/party venue/
barbeque garden/personal museum operating on the site of a former
car wash and café. Larry Meeks, the owner of the site, also owned a
nearby auto styling salon. Meeks purchased the site of the Car Wash
Café to use as a storage facility for cars that he was in the process of
repairing. He introduced a car wash that employed teenagers from the
surrounding neighborhood and, when customers of the car wash and
neighborhood residents began to congregate at the car wash, opened
an ice-cream stand to provide refreshments and a place to spend time.
The stand eventually became a sit-down café, which spilled over into
the adjacent auto storage facility, sponsoring the transformation of the
latter into a barbeque garden. The explicit programming of the site was
complemented by its use as a space to display the objects that Meeks
collected, which comprised a rich cross-section of auto-related urban
ephemera: cars, car parts, gas pumps, signal lights, roadside signs
and so on.

Meek's ability to utilize his urban site without concern for profit making
allowed its functions to emerge and transform over the course of
time through a series of *improvisational programs*. Moreover, these
programs, and the equipment that supported them, were themselves

collected in the Car Wash Café, so that the site also served as a
museum of its own history. The signs and advertisements that filled the
site publicized not a current reality, but layers of the past—a historical
project that was all the more powerful by not being marked as such.
The Car Wash Café was, at once, abandoned, completed, musealized
and waiting to re-open for the next party.

Patrimony of the Unlost
# African Bead Museum

The African Bead Museum was founded by artist and curator Olayame Dabls as a repository of the African culture that many African Americans have been separated from, first by slavery and then by other forms of social, cultural and political oppression. The museum collects and displays African beads along with sculpture, textiles, pottery, metalwork and other African material culture. The museum preserves a cultural patrimony for its potential heirs, yet it also actively reappropriates that patrimony as a resource for contemporary cultural production.

For twenty years before the museum was founded, Dabls assembled its collection in the context of a bead gallery; the gallery moved nomadically through Detroit, occupying the Book Tower, Trapper's Alley and the David Whitney Building in turn. In 1994, Dabls founded the museum and in 1998 he moved it into a large building, donated to him, on Detroit's near Westside. This building also came to house American Black Artists, an organization founded by Leno Jaxon, first director of the Charles Wright Museum of African American History, where Dabls had worked as a curator.

Dabls surfaced the exterior walls of the museum in broken mirrors, paintings and painted wood, an assemblage of materials and forms that draws from and transforms various African architectural traditions. In 2008, Dabls was given another building adjacent to the museum; told by city authorities that this building had to be closed until it was restored, Dabls re-purposed the building's closure by surfacing the building with mirrors, woods and paint and framing it as a Congolese fetish object, or N'kisi, endowed with powers to both sicken and heal.

Between the museum and N'kisi, in a space formerly used to dump debris, Dabls also built a series of installations out of debris and other found objects. The largest installation, entitled "Iron Teaching Rocks to Rust," is a *material narrative* about the historical process of Europeanization that African slaves and their descendents were compelled to undergo. Here, as on the walls of the museum and N'kisi, Dabls has appropriated unutilized urban property as a place of memory, mourning and cultural reclamation.

Patrimony of the Unlost
# Heidelberg Project

At the Heidelberg Project, artist Tyree Guyton appropriates abandoned houses and vacant lots on Detroit's Eastside as sites for the display of made and found objects. Guyton, who grew up in a house on a block of Heidelberg Street, collects and exhibits objects from the detritus he finds in and around his neighborhood: stuffed animals, vacuum cleaners, television sets, shoes, hubcaps, telephones and other items of domestic urban life. According to Guyton, the project's original agenda emerged as a defamiliarization of what was conventionally perceived to be mere garbage: "there was no plan and no blueprint, just the will and determination to see beauty in the refuse." The waste objects of this *oppositional aestheticization* are carefully curated, arrayed on empty lots or hung from the walls of abandoned houses or trees. These objects are often decorated with colored polka dots, which also adorn houses, cars, trees and street surfaces on and around the site of the project.

The Heidelberg Project appropriates both abandoned objects and abandoned property. The latter appropriation could also be framed as "squatting," or illegal occupation, and the City of Detroit has twice destroyed parts of the project, in 1991 and 1999, in response to protests from local community organizations.

These protests contradicted, to some degree, Guyton's expressed
intention "to improve lives and neighborhoods through art." Yet, what
and where is "the community?" Who can legitimately speak on behalf of
the community? Who is able to listen to the community? How can art
benefit the community? The Heidelberg Project raises these complex
questions without providing simple answers in response, a provocation
particularly suited to unreal estate and one that may yet comprise the
project's most profound social effect.

# Glossary

**Active Neglect:** the deliberate withholding of investment and other resources from Detroit's predominantly African-American neighborhoods on the part of both business and government, especially in the post-World War II decades, as a result of both structural racism and economic restructuring; a causal factor in the production of <u>unreal estate</u>. Reference: Thomas J. Sugrue, *The Origins of the Urban Crisis: Race and Inequality in Postwar Detroit* (Princeton: Princeton University Press, 1997).

**Blight Tourism:** tourism focused on derelict buildings, abandoned neighborhoods and other apparent signs of urban blight, the putative products of <u>Detroitification</u>; a conventional means of misapprehending <u>unreal estate</u>.

**Blots:** from "block" and "lot," the space formed by the expansion of a single-family house lot into an adjacent abandoned lot; the building block of <u>new suburbanism</u>. Reference: Tobias Armborst, Daniel D'Oca and Georgeen Theodore, "Improve Your Lot!" in *Cities Growing Smaller*, 1 (2008), 45-64.

**Cass Corridor:** inner-city neighborhood adjacent to Wayne State University and bisected by Cass Avenue; a site of vibrant art-making and art-exhibiting scenes and related countercultural activities from the 1960s through 80s; a preliminary site of <u>unreal estate</u> speculation.

**Charrette:** an event at which architects and urban planners come to Detroit and, in consultation with local stakeholders typically drawn from business, government and community organizations, labor intensively over a short period of time in a securitized workplace to produce design proposals for large-scale municipal development; a means for architects and planners to engage with <u>unreal estate</u> as empty space.

**Crackhead-to-Artist Ratio:** statistic used to evaluate the progress of <u>gentrification</u>, either in the context of celebrating <u>gentrification</u> or protesting against it.

**Creative Class:** from liberal perspectives, a socioeconomic population whose work privileges creativity and innovation and drives urban economic development; from radical perspectives, an objective abstraction that is used to legitimize neoliberal economic restructuring, gentrification and other forms of violence against the urban poor and disenfranchised.

**Deconstruction:** the disassembly of buildings slated for destruction in order to preserve and recycle their components; an alternative to demolition and demolitionism.

**Demolitionism:** Detroit's official model of urban renewal which proceeds through demolition as opposed to construction or deconstruction; especially apparent in Detroit's Central Business District, where many abandoned buildings have been demolished to make way for parking lots. See parking empire.

**Desire Line** (also "desire path" and "social trail"): path created by foot-traffic across a field, usually the shortest distance between a point of departure and destination; in Detroit, a common feature on supposedly "vacant" lots. Reference: Gaston Bachelard, *The Poetics of Space* (Boston: Beacon Press, 1969) and Jim Griffioen, "Streets With No Name," http://www.sweetjuniper .com/2009/06/streets-with-no-name.html.

**Detro:** from "SoHo" and "Detroit," a potential product of artist-led gentrification in Detroit, along the lines of New York's SoHo, imagined by some artists and their supporters; criticized from anti-gentrification perspectives as foreclosing on the cultural, social and political possibilities emerging from capitalist underdevelopment. Reference: Andrew Herscher, "From SoHo to Detro?" *Detroit Free Press*, April 1, 2009.

**Detroit Dacha:** from the Russian "dacha" (second home located in a rural area); a home on an otherwise abandoned block that avails itself of that block's landscape, solitude and other qualities and thereby complicates narratives of urban decline or ruination.

**Detroitification:** massive urban decline, on the order of the process that is conventionally understood to have taken place in Detroit; a perception of urban ruin and a neglect of urban creativity that collaborates in the production of the problematic situation it seemingly only describes.

**Detroitland**: fantasy-image of Detroit as a business friendly, culturally rich and well governed city crafted by municipal government to enhance Detroit's ability to secure investment, tourism and business services in competitive global economy. Compare with Detroitification.

**Dirty Dozen**: twelve abandoned buildings in downtown Detroit posited by urban explorers as targets for exploration; a critical re-framing of the twelve "Towers of Neglect" posed by the *Detroit Free Press* as signs of the city's dereliction.

**Everyday Urbanism**: an informal production of urban space that is posed as an alternative urbanism, opposed or resistant to hegemonic urban culture.

**Feral House**: an abandoned house that has been colonized by plants and animals and therefore rendered as an undomesticated site. See Jim Griffioen, "Feral Houses," http://www.sweetjuniper.com/2009/07/feral-houses.html.

**Food Desert**: the territory occupied by central Detroit's low-income residents, who lack easy access to grocery stores; a condition that solicits alternative forms of food production and food consumption and thus new forms of self-determination in the preceding.

**Gentrification**: the process that converts unreal estate into real estate, often utilizing artists, architects, designers and other professionals who need inexpensive property; a means to colonize supposedly decrepit neighborhoods and support the conversion of those neighborhoods into investment-friendly environments. See creative class.

**Ghetto**: the object of gentrification; an urban space where, due to active neglect, economic opportunities, investment, security, infrastructure and municipal services have been withheld; also an urban space where cultural, social, economic and political alternatives to dominant capitalist and liberal structures can be imagined and practiced.

**Ghetto Bee**: honey bee from an urban colony, which in Detroit are often located on vacant lots or urban gardens, sites of unintended biodiversity that are very conducive to beekeeping.

**Ghetto Palm:** common term for *Ailanthis altissima*, a rapidly growing and aggressively spreading deciduous tree, found on roofs and interiors of abandoned buildings throughout Detroit, which easily withstands polluted soil and can colonize areas which other plants cannot tolerate.

**Ghetto Tech** (sp. also "Ghettotech," "Geto Tek" and "Ghettotec"; compare with Detroit Bass, Booty Bass and Booty Music): a form of electronic dance music, drawing from ghetto house, electro, hip hop and techno, that originated in Detroit and is showcased in the annual Detroit Electronic Music Festival; a recuperation of urban dereliction as a site of creative cultural production.

**Green:** the color of "sustainability" in environments framed as economically valuable; the color of "dereliction" in environments framed as economically valueless.

**Landlord Nation:** the post-foreclosure housing environment in Detroit, where owner-occupied houses have become increasingly scarce.

**Motor City** (similar to Motown): term for Detroit that references the city's status in the early and mid 20th century as center of the American automotive industry; usually used nostalgically, ironically or promotionally. Compare with: <u>Motor Shitty</u>.

**Motor Shitty:** term for Detroit that references the city's post-industrial decline, usually used affectionately and ironically. Compare with: <u>Motor City</u>.

**New Suburbanism:** process by which entrepreneurial home-owners in inner-city Detroit appropriate adjacent vacant lots and thereby amass suburban-scale parcels of land, or "blots"; a means to accomplish "creative shrinkage" or "smart downsizing." Reference: Interboro Partners, "However Unspectacular: The New Suburbanism," in *Shrinking Cities*, vol. 2, ed. Philp Oswalt (Ostfildern: Hatje Cantz, 2006).

**Open City:** the name of a 1960s era countercultural initiative on <u>Cass Corridor</u> providing a range of services, including crash pad, free clinic, free store and suicide hotline; also the name of an early 21st century business initiative networking aspiring entrepreneurs in Detroit; a figure for the recuperation of cultural critique as marketing strategy in late capitalism.

**Parking Empire:** expanding system of parking lots in downtown Detroit owned by billionaire Mike Ilitch, created by destroying buildings to make parking for Detroit-based athletic events; a conversion of architectural spaces into parking spaces that may represent the final moment of the city's auto-privileged urbanization. See: demolitionism.

**Poverty:** from dehistoricized perspectives, the product of bad choices or moral deficiencies on the part of individuals; from historically inflected perspectives, the product of structural discrimination against or oppression of entire communities.

**Prozac Tour:** synonym for blight tour; can apply to condition of tour audience, which is depressed by the dereliction of Detroit, and tour guide, who is depressed by the narrow-mindedness of many suburban audience members. See: blight tourism.

**Rebellion:** term for collective urban violence in Detroit in the 1960s that politicizes that violence and casts it as an authorized disruption of an oppressive and violent regime of order. Compare with: riot.

**Renaissance:** term for neoliberal transformation of Detroit through privatization, gentrification and securitization, used by advocates of that transformation to cast it as a natural and objective public good.

**Riot:** term for collective urban violence in Detroit in the 1960s that depoliticizes that violence and casts it as an unauthorized disruption of a legitimate regime of social and political order. Compare with: rebellion.

**Ruin Porn:** images of derelict buildings in Detroit, posed in many media accounts of Detroit as representative of the condition of the city itself. Reference: Thomas Morton, "Something, Something, Something, Detroit: Lazy Journalists Love Pictures of Abandoned Stuff," *Vice* 16:8 (2009).

**Scrapping:** scavenging metal, such as copper, nickel and brass, from abandoned buildings, usually practiced by homeless or impoverished men; metal is typically transported via shopping carts to scrap yards, where it is purchased by the pound. Reference: Scott Hocking, "Scrappers," in *Shrinking Cities*, vol. 1, ed. Philp Oswalt (Ostfildern: Hatje Cantz, 2005).

**Skimming**: the salvaging of easy-to-remove materials from buildings slated for destruction; a legal alternative to scrapping that can yield economic value for both the skimmer, who can re-sell skimmed material, and the skimmee, who can receive a tax deduction for material skimmed by a non-profit organization.

**Unreal Estate**: property that loses exchange value to the point where it can assume use values that are unrecognized by or prohibited in the property regime; a waste product of capitalist development; a resource for claiming a right to the city.

**Urbanism**: the formation of the city according to the imperatives of capitalist development, often as translated into professional expertise, political agendas or cultural ideology.

**White Flight**: the departure of whites from Detroit to surrounding suburbs, widespread after World War II, to avoid living in proximity to the city's African-American population; both contributing to and produced by the active neglect of the city's African-American neighborhoods.

**White Fly-Over**: post-white flight return of white suburbanites or tourists to Detroit for cultural or sporting events, urban exploration or other temporary "low-risk" occupations.

# References

**African Bead Museum**
www.mbad.org.

DeAndra Mack, "African Beads Cultivate Cultures, Community," **Michigan Citizen**, http://michigancitizen.com/african-beads-cultivate-cultures-community-p3367-73.htm.

"Mirror Man," http://www.detroitblog.org/?p=499.

—

**Alley Culture**
http://72.29.73.163/~vox/ac.

David Little, "Colab Takes a Piece, History Takes It Back: Collectivity and New York Alternative Spaces," *Art Journal* 66:1 (2007), 60–74.

—

**Architectural Salvage Warehouse**
http://www.aswdetroit.org/index.htm

Nick Sousanis, "Architectural Salvage Warehouse of Detroit," *The Detroiter*, 8 June 2006.

—

**Blotting**

Tobias Armborst, Daniel D'Oca and Georgeen Theodore, "Improve Your Lot!" in *Cities Growing Smaller*, 1 (2008), 45-64.

Tobias Armborst, Daniel D'Orca and Georgeen Theodore, "However Unspectacular," in *Shrinking Cities: Interventions*, ed. Philipp Oswalt (Ostfildern-Ruit, Germany: Hatje Cantz Verlag, 2006).

—

**Boggs Center**
http://www.boggscenter.org.

Grace Lee Boggs, with Scott Kurashige, *The Next American Revolution: Sustainable Activism for the Twenty-First Century.* Berkeley: University of California Press, 2011.

James Boggs, *Pages From a Black Radical's Notebook: A James Boggs Reader.* Detroit: Wayne State University Press, 2011.

—

**Brightmoor Farmway**

Jon Kalish, "Farming Detroit," *Makezine*, September 2011, http://blog.makezine.com/archive/2011/09/farming-detroit.html.

—

**Car Wash Café**

Michael Jackman, "Car Wash Café Owner Dead at 56," *Metro Times*, 18 May 2010.

Sarah Klein, "One Man's Trash," *Metro Times*, 7 June 2005.

—

**Catherine Ferguson Academy**
http://detroitk12.org/schools/school/742.

http://defendpubliceducation.com.

Lisa M. Collins, "School of Life," *Metro Times*, 24 November 2004.

—

**Center for Creative eXchange**
http://www.centerforcreativeXchange.org.

http://ccxchange.blogspot.com.

—

**Contemporary Art Institute of Detroit**
http://www.status1.org/caid.

Nick Sousanis, "Charles McGee: Metamorphosis and Kinetic Energy," *The Detroiter*, http://www.thedetroiter.com/nov04/mcgee.html.

—

**D-Town Farm**
http://detroitblackfoodsecurity.org.

Malik Yakini, "Undoing Racism in the Detroit Food System," *Michigan Citizen*, 21 December 2010.

Jenny Lee and Paul Abowd, "Detroit's Grassroots Economies," *In These Times*, 17 March 2011.

"Detroit Urban Agriculture Movement Looks to Reclaim Motor City," *Democracy Now*, 24 June 2010, http://www.democracynow.org/2010/6/24/detroit_urban_agriculture_movement_looks_to_reclaim_motor_city.

—

**Dally in the Alley**
http://www.dallyinthealley.com.

—

**Detroit Blues**
http://detroiturbex.com.

"The Big Twelve—Detroit's Towers of Neglect," *Detroit Free Press*, 18 May 2004.

—

**Detroit Demolition Disneyland**

"Detroit Demolition Disneyland," *The Detroiter*, http://www.thedetroiter.com/nov05/disneydemolition.php.

Marisol Bello, "Look at Blight, Color Shouts," *Detroit Free Press*, 6 March 2006.

Rebecca Mazzei, "An Object Orange Alert," *Metro Times*, 19-25 April 2006.

—

**Detroit Geographical Expedition**

Andy Merrifield, "Situated Knowledge Through Exploration: Reflections on Bunge's 'Geographical Expeditions,'" *Antipodes* 27:1 (1995).

—

**Detroit Guerrilla Queer Bar**
http://www.detroitguerrillas.com.

—

**Detroit Industrial Gallery**
http://www.detroitindustrialgallery.com.

—

**Detroit Unreal Estate Agency**

Lee Rodney, "Detroit is Our Future," *Fuse* 32:4 (2009).

Toby Barlow, "For Sale: The $100 House," *New York Times*, 7 March 2009.

"Atlas of Love and Hate," *Volume 22* (2010).

—

**Earthworks Urban Farm**
http://www.cskdetroit.org/EWG.

Olga Bonfiglio, "Growing Green in Detroit," *Christian Science Monitor*, 21 August 2008.

—

**Field of Our Dreams**
http://fieldofourdreams.ning.com/.

Nick Tobier, "Field of Our Dreams, *Fuse* 35:3 (2010).

—

**Filter Detroit**
http://www.filter-hamburg.com/en/

—

**FireBreak**

Dan Pitera, "FireBreak: Architecture and Community Agitation," http://arch.udmercy.edu/dc/De_Sign-Firebreak-Intro.html

—

**Georgia Street Community Garden**
http://georgiastreetgarden.blogspot.com.

Gabe Nelson, "Urban Farming Puts Down Roots," *Crain's Detroit Business*, 23 August 2009.

Larry Gabriel, "Body vs. Soul Food," *Metro Times*, 4-10 January 2012.

—

**Greening of Detroit**
http://www.greeningofdetroit.com.

Elizabeth DiNovella, "The Greening of Detroit," *The Progressive*, 23 June 2010.

Tom Philpott, "From Motown to Growtown: The Greening of Detroit," *Grist*, 24 August 2010.

—

**Hamtramck Disneyland**

Jack Lessenberry, "Hamtramck Disneyland," *Metro Times*, 15 January 2003.

Walter Wasacz, "Unofficial Art," *Model D*, 15 August 2006.

—

**Heidelberg Project**
http://www.heidelberg.org.

Tyree Guyton, *Connecting the Dots: Tyree Guyton's Heidelberg Project*. Detroit: Wayne State University Press, 2007.

—

**Hookie Monsters**
http://detroiturbex.com.

Chastity Pratt Dawsey, "DPS Increases School Closures to 20 in Latest Plan," *Detroit Free Press*, 27 May 2011.

—

**Hope District**

Eric T. Campbell, "Hope District: True Community Development Spreads One Block at a Time," *Michigan Citizen*, http://michigancitizen.com/hope-district-p6206-1.htm.

Larry Gabriel, "Hope Lives Here," *Metro Times*, 3 December 2008.

—

**Hygienic Dress League**
http://www.hygienicdressleague.com.

Donna Terek, "Street Artists Put Unique Brand on Detroit," *Detroit News*, 14 November 2010.

—

**John's Carpet House**
http://www.johnscarpethouse.com.

Louis Aguilar, "John's Carpet House a Piece of 'Detroit Soul'," *Detroit News*, 5 July 2009.

—

**The Lot**
http://thelotdetroit.blogspot.com/

—

**Michigan Building Parking Garage**

Dan Austin, *Lost Detroit: Stories Behind the Motor City's Majestic Ruins*. Charleston, SC: History Press, 2010.

Vivian M. Baulch, "Detroit's Fabulous Michigan Theatre," *Detroit News*, 17 March 2001.

—

**Motor City Blight Busters**
http://www.blightbusters.org.

Curt Guyette, "Blight Buster," *Metro Times*, 11 June 2008.

—

**Peacemakers International**
http://www.peacemakersinternational.org.

Detroitblogger John, "Desolation Angel," *Metro Times*, 26 January 2011.

—

**Peaches and Greens**
http://www.centraldetroitchristian.org/Peaches_and_Greens_Market.htm.

Eric T. Campbell, "Small Grocery Store Delivers Large Benefits," *Michigan Citizen*, http://michigancitizen.com/small-grocery-store-delivers-large-benefits-p7117-1.htm.

Jonathan Oosting, "Peaches and Greens Brings Healthy Eating Options to Detroit," *Mlive.com*, 11 August 2009.

—

**Pink Pony Express**
http://pinkponyexpress.blogspot.com.

—

**Power House**
http://www.powerhouseproject.com.

Walter Wasacz, "Detroit House: $100. Bold New Ideas for the City: Priceless," *Model D*, 17 March 2009.

Kelli B. Kavanaugh, "Art into Action: Design Collaborators Building Community One Power House at a Time," *Model D*, 30 November 2010.

—

**Salvaged Landscape**
http://cathlynnewell.com/Salvaged-Landscape.

Zev Chafets, *Devil's Night and Other True Tales of Detroit* (New York: Random House, 1990).

—

**Secret Pizza Party**

Chris Handyside, "Reaching 'The Whole Why World'," *Metro Times*, 19 April 2006.

—

**Seed Detroit**
http://seeddetroit.blogspot.com.

—

**Submerge**
http://www.submerge.com.

C. Vecchiola, "Submerge in Detroit: Techno's Creative Response to Urban Crisis," *Journal of American Studies*, 45 (2011).

—

**Tashmoo Biergarten**
http://tashmoodetroit.com.

—

**Theatre Bizzare**
http://www.theatrebizarre.com.

Mary M. Chapman, "Detroit Reins in an Annual Holiday Party," *New York Times*, 29 October 2010.

Michael Jackman, "Fright Club," *Metro Times*, 29 October 2003.

—

**Tree of Heaven Woodshop**
http://www.treeofheavenwoodshop.com.

—

**Trumbullplex**
http://trumbullplex.org.

http://www.myspace.com/trumbullplex.

Dominique Osborne, "Radically Wholesome," *Metro Times*, 11 September 2002.

"Spirit Infusion," *Alley Culture News*, Fall 2003.

—

**UFO Factory**
http://ufofactory.com.

http://www.myspace.com/ufofactory.

Jennifer Andrews, "UFOs Land in Detroit: Art Scene May Never Be the Same," *Model D*, 8 July 2008.

—

**Yes Farm**
http://theyesfarm.blogspot.com.

Michael Jackman, "Just Say Yes," *Metro Times*, 5 May 2010.

Melena Ryzik, "Wringing Art Out of the Rubble in Detroit," *New York Times*, 3 August 2010.

—

# Acknowledgments

This book emerged from a collective endeavor. It was inspired by discussions within the Detroit Unreal Estate Agency; I thank Christian Ernsten, Femke Lutgerink and Mireille Roddier, as well as all others who came to participate in the Agency's activities.

The development of this book would have been both unthinkable and impossible without the thoughts and ideas that many people in and around Detroit graciously shared with me. I am particularly grateful for conversations with KT Andresky, Mike Banks, Annemarie van den Berg, Grace Lee Boggs, Steve Coy, Mark Covington, Olayame Dabls, Kate Daughdrill, Margi Dewar, Eric Dueweke, Tyree Guyton, Scott Hocking, Garrett MacLean, Melanie Manos, Larry Meeks, Chazz Miller, Kerstin Niemann, Dan Pitera, Lee Rodney, Dmytro Szylak, Greg Tom, Nick Tobier, Etienne Turpin, Corine Vermeulen, Volcano, Craig Wilkins and Mike Wimberley, among many others.

I not only benefited from Garrett MacLean's generous contribution of several beautiful photographs to this book, but also from an ongoing conversation with him about visualizing an unreal city. Catie Newell also kindly contributed several of her remarkable photographs.

At the University of Michigan, the work of the Detroit Unreal Estate Agency was supported by Theresa Reid, Executive Director of the Arts on Earth Program, and Tom Buresh, former Chair of the Architecture Program at the Taubman College of Architecture and Urban Planning. The generous support of Monica Ponce de Leon, Dean of the Taubman College, was vital to the completion of this book.

At the University of Michigan Press, I am grateful for Tom Dwyer's steadfast belief in this book. Comments on the manuscript from the Press's anonymous readers, as well as from Margi Dewar, Danny Herwitz and Claire Zimmerman, were also very helpful. Tirtza Even's last-minute interventions were more than welcome; they were crucial. Marc Maxey helped me conceive the design of the book; this design was expertly realized, in every sense, by Christian Unverzagt.

I dedicate this book to my sister and brother, in gratitude for their unreal love.

# Image Credits

All images are by the author except the following, which are authored and copyrighted by:

253 (Alley Culture small) Melanie Manos; 254-255 (Alley Culture large) Luna Dizon; 155-157 (Block Clubbing) Amanda Olczak; 233 (Blotting small) Interboro Partners; 234-235 (Blotting large) Kate Davidson, Changing Gears/ Michigan Radio; 53-55 (Brightmoor Farmway) Nora Mandray/detroitjetaime. com; 152-153 (Catherine Ferguson Academy large) Creative Commons; 209 (Center for Creative eXchange small) Center for Creative eXchange; 269 (Contemporary Art Institute of Detroit small) Creative Commons; 164-165 (Dally in the Alley large) Eugene Wicke; 45-47 (D-Town Farm) Creative Commons; 89-91 (Detroit Blues) Detroit Blues; 27-29 (Detroit Demolition Disneyland) Object Orange courtesy of Paul Kotula Projects; 109-111 (Detroit Geographical Expedition) Alibi Studio; 171 (Detroit Guerrilla Queer Bar small) Ally Lindsay; 239 (Detroit Industrial Gallery small) Creative Commons; 84-85 (Detroit Mower Gang large) Nora Mandray/detroitjetaime.com; 83 (Detroit Mower Gang small) Tom Nardone/Detroit Mower Gang; 4-5 (Detroit Unreal Estate Agency large) Corine Vermeulen; 217-219 (Ego Circus) Ego Circus; 41-43 (Earthworks Urban Farm) Earthworks Urban Farm; 195 (Farnsworth Street small) Pink Pony Express; 196-197 (Farnsworth Street large) Garrett MacLean; 61-63 (Field of Our Dreams) Nick Tobier; 31-33 (FireBreak) Dan Pitera/ Detroit Collaborative Design Center; 200-201 (Fourth Street large) Nora Mandray/detroitjetaime.com; 127-129 (Friends of Gorgeous Berries) James D. Griffioen; 244-245 (Full Scale Design Lab large) Catie Newell; 93-95 (Hookie Monsters) Hookie Monsters; 261 (The Lot small) Garrett Maclean; 262-263 (The Lot large) Kathy Leisen; 229 (Peacemakers small) Pink Pony Express; 57-59 (Peaches and Greens) Pink Pony Express; 113 (Pink Pony Express small) Garrett MacLean; 114-115 (Pink Pony Express large) Pink Pony Express; 35-37 (Salvaged Landscape) Catie Newell; 137 (Secret Pizza Party small) Andy DeGiulio/solidbrass.org; 180-181 (Tashmoo Biergarten large) Marvin Shaouni; 141-143 (Trtl) Erika Lindsay; 185 (UFO Factory small) UFO Factory; 186-187 (UFO Factory large) Marvin Shaouni; 97 (Urban Yoga Lab small) Garrett Maclean; 98-99 (Urban Yoga Lab large) Kaleena Quinn; 189-191 (Yes Farm) KT Andresky/Yes Farm

# WONDERFUL WAYS
## *to* BE *a*
# STEPPARENT

# WONDERFUL WAYS
## *to* BE *a*
# STEPPARENT

*Judy Ford* and *Anna Chase*

CONARI PRESS
Berkeley, California

*Cover illustration:* Lisa Burnett Bossi,
Fineline Marketing and Design

*Cover art direction:* Ame Beanland

*Cover and interior design:* Suzanne Albertson

Conari Press books are distributed by Publishers Group West.

ISBN: 1-57324-147-4

**Library of Congress Cataloging-in-Publication Data**
Ford, Judy.
Wonderful ways to be a stepparent / Judy Ford and Anna Chase.
p.      cm.
ISBN 1-57324-147-4 (tradepaper)
1. Stepparents. 2. Stepfamilies. I. Chase, Anna. II. Title.
HQ759.92.F67   1999                    98–44203
306.874—dc21                              CIP

Printed in the United States of America on recycled paper
99 00 01 02  RRD(C) 1 2 3 4 5 6 7 8 9 10

*Wonderful Ways to Be a Stepparent*

## DEALING WITH YOUR SPOUSE

## INTERACTING WITH THE KIDS

# Acknowledgments

Thanks to Alex Witchel, whose *Girls Only* gave us the inspiration for the unspoken "I Love You"s.

## FROM ANNA:

I want to give special thanks to Judy Ford for allowing me to share her "wonderful ways" format. I'd been searching for the right way to write about stepparenting for twenty years, and it wasn't until I saw her *Wonderful Ways to Love a Child* that I realized how to do it. Judy was gracious and generous enough to allow me to do this book with her.

Many conversations with stepparents and kids inform the pages of this book. I want to thank particularly Ann, Marilyn, Dawna, and Andy. I also want to thank, from the bottom of my heart, the angel, Daphne, who helped me through every stage and phase of the stepparenting process—I couldn't have done it without you.

Most of all, I want to thank my stepchildren, who appear in these pages as Michael and Zoe to protect their privacy. We have been in one another's lives now for twenty years, and much of who I am now is a result of the experiences we've had together. Thanks for being in my life.

## FROM JUDY:

It is an enormously generous act by my daughter, Amanda, to allow me to write about her. I am eternally grateful for her presence in my life and in these pages.

I want to thank the many stepfamilies whom I've met in my parenting classes and as clients for the privilege of hammering out with them a new model for stepparenting.

And finally, my deepest appreciation to Conari Press, the publisher of all my books, for their ongoing commitment to my work.

## *Once Upon a Time*

The finest gift you can give
to your spouse and stepchildren
is the gift of gentle healing—
showing them that even after one family splits up,
you can *all* come together as an expanded clan.

You meet someone and fall in love—he's perfect in every way. Oh, and he has two kids from a former marriage who live with him half-time. No problem, you think. We love each other, so we can work out whatever issues the kids present. Right!

How many of us enter stepparenting totally blind, completely unaware of the pitfalls, problems, and difficulties ahead? Virtually all of us, we would venture to say. "I certainly was unaware of the challenges twenty years ago when a man and his two children, aged six months and two-and-a-half, came into my life," recalls Anna. "I remember thinking, 'Well, I like kids, so why not?' When we began to hit various bumps in the road—his son wanted nothing to do with me, his ex-wife broke into our house and destroyed my clothes—I was surprised. Shocked even. This was hard!"

No one can be prepared in advance for the roller coaster of experiences and emotions from all sides of blended families—yours, his, your kids, his kids, the in-laws, the ex-in-laws, the ex-spouse(s).... Marriage and kids are hard enough, without adding the complexities of all those psyches, each potentially brewing up a batch of anger, resentment, and bitterness.

But stepparenting doesn't have to be all hell and hard work. Not that it isn't hard—(every single stepparent we spoke with admitted that the role was harder than they had expected)—but it can be easier with a bit of knowledge and a set of new attitudes. And sometimes, maybe often, maybe not, it can even be a source of joy and happiness. No matter what, it is always an opportunity for soul growth—yours, your spouse's, and the kids'. For, no matter how hard it gets, you are in their lives for a reason, as they are in yours.

"Twenty years ago, when I hit the skids of stepparenting," says Anna, "I sought advice in books, but didn't find anything truly useful. It was all too negative, or superficial and Pollyannaish. What you are holding in your hands now is the advice I wished I had then. It comes from two decades of my own experience and lots of conversations with other stepparents, combined with the positive 'parenting with love and laughter' approach of Judy Ford."

It is not our intention to sugarcoat the process of creating a blended family. But we do believe strongly that if you acknowledge the realities of the situation to yourself, your spouse, kids, and stepkids, and accentuate the positive on the day-to-day level, you can have a wonderful relationship with your stepchildren and live in a house full of love and laughter.

*Wonderful Ways to Be a Stepparent* is a prescription to strengthen your family. The book is filled with stories of stepparents who are building strong, loving new families, and offers more than sixty suggestions for dealing with everything from money and discipline to having more fun together. To really make these ideas work, you'll need compassion—for yourself, your spouse, and the children in your care—and all the emotional honesty you can muster.

To thrive, every child needs love, trust, respect, and acceptance, and the more adults who can provide these essential elements, the better. In the end, the labels *mother, father, stepmother, stepfather* matter less than the quality of our interactions with the young ones entrusted to our care. We stepparents have been give a precious opportunity to offer our love, trust, respect, and acceptance to the young souls who have entered our lives.

Stepparents are on a mission of hope and healing. When one family is separated by divorce or death, another family composition emerges. In time, the new family synthesis is often wiser, more compassionate, and rich with experience. It takes years to build a family history, years to have a happy ending, but it's worth the effort, because when you look back on your life together you'll discover it's chock-full of incredible human experiences. Your family history will be full of stories of healing, tears and laughter, and trials and triumphs that you'll all be retelling for years to come. These stories make you a family.

Stepparents arrive on the scene full of hope, bearing unspoken promises of fresh beginnings and renewal, promises of creating an expanded, richly textured family unit. By remembering this no matter what is happening, you will find that being a stepparent can be wonderful indeed, and that you can live happily together.

# RELATING TO YOURSELF

*The best reformers the world
has ever seen are those who
commence on themselves.*

—George Bernard Shaw

# OPEN YOUR HEART

Opening your heart to your stepchild may be very easy for you—or very difficult. It depends on the particulars of the situation and the personalities involved. But it is possible to do, even under the most trying circumstances, if you can engage your compassion.

Compassion is the ability to "feel with" someone else, to enter into his or her experience and recognize their pain. It's compassion we feel when we see a picture of children starving in Sudan and send money to CARE. It's compassion we experience when we notice a tired look on our beloved's face and offer to do the dishes.

We shouldn't be afraid of compassion for our stepchildren out of fear that they will "take advantage" of us. Rather, we should practice opening our hearts to them every day, if only in private, so that our compassion for their suffering can help us weather the rough spots in our relationship.

Everyone wants and needs to be loved—and that includes both you and the children who have come into your sphere of influence as a consequence of your relationship with their parent. You are probably aware of your desire for them to love, or at least have warm feelings, toward you. You want them to like you, to accept you, to treat you well, and to enjoy being in your company.

They, on the other hand, may be overtly needy of love, mouths wide open like baby birds waiting for worms, or as defensive and hostile as the most surly teenager is capable of. But don't let outward appearances fool you—no matter who your stepchild is, he or she longs to be known and appreciated. And no matter what situation you find yourself in, make no mistake in recognizing that your stepchild is as least as angry and scared as you—and with less experience in dealing with such strong feelings.

So there they are in front of you, with at *least* the intensity of emotions you are experiencing. They have not been on the Earth very long and have been through a lot already—the divorce or death of a parent; maybe several "potential stepparents" when Mom or Dad was dating; perhaps even a stepparent or two already. If we are willing to feel compassion toward these young souls, our hearts will naturally open as we empathetically relate to the suffering they have already gone through, the confusion they must be feeling right now. And when our hearts are open, our love will flow more freely— regardless of their ability to receive it in the moment.

# GIVE UP YOUR DREAM OF
# THE PERFECT FAMILY

Do you have an image of the perfect family? Chances are it comes from television. Depending on your age, it might be the Cleavers from *Leave It to Beaver*, the Keatons from *Family Ties*, or the Huxtables from *Cosby*. No matter which, these were all "intact" families with parents who loved each other well and communicated perfectly, and kids who, despite minor squabbles, got along heart-warmingly with one another and ultimately always took their parents' advice. These paragon families always celebrated Christmas and birthdays together, and went on happy family vacations.

In shape and substance, these media families probably bear little resemblance to the kind of family structure you now find yourself in. This can be hard. When we set ourselves up for a particular circumstance and it doesn't come to pass, we can get so focused on what we don't have that we can fail to appreciate what we do have. In particular, the nuclear family is a very potent archetype, which means it is locked into our deep unconscious as a model of how family life should be. When in reality we experience something different, there can be profound sadness or anger.

Rachel remembers how hard it was for her to come to terms with

# DO A TWO-MINUTE
# REALITY CHECK

Remember the old adage—the truth will set you free? However you expected your family life to be before you got married, chances are your expectation doesn't match up to reality. That's why one of the first steps in making stepparenting wonderful is to let go of all the expectations of the way you thought it would—or should—be, and take a realistic look at the way things are. What this means is that either in a journal or a private conversation with yourself, take two minutes a day to do an inventory of the way things are. Not the way you wish they were or hope they could be, but what truly is: I'm having more trouble adjusting to life with kids than I thought I would; I'm angry Fred is feeling so guilty about the divorce that he is spoiling his kids and I'm afraid to talk to him about it; I'm hurt that little Emily is wary of me and Dylan is downright hostile.

It's really important that you just take note of the way things really are without judgment: I'm angry; I'm hurt; I'm feeling rejected. What's important about this judgment-free assessment is that it allows you to come out of denial and really face the truth of what's going on. This is not easy to do. Anna remembers that it took her a couple of years to admit that she was not happy about sharing her husband with her stepkids. "It just seemed so selfish and petty," she her new family. "For years, I constantly felt like the fifth wheel. The kids would arrive for a week, eager to see their dad. I was an afterthought. Whenever we would meet their friends, he would get introduced, but not me. I was irrelevant. And they never made me a Mother's Day card or gave me a birthday present. It was so painful, partly I guess because I had pictured us as *The Waltons* or something. When I finally stopped wishing it were different and made peace with the fact that we are a complex family that has a lot of issues to deal with, things got better. I stopped waiting for the birthday card and wishing for the Hallmark family moments, and lightened up. Miraculously, the kids felt the lack of pressure and actually got warmer toward me."

Your family is as unique as you are, and it is only because the Cleavers, the Huxtables, and the Keatons are fictional that their families are "perfect." Every family has its own difficulties and beauty. By giving up on an image of how it *should* be, you take a great step toward making it as good as it *can* be.

They, on the other hand, may be overtly needy of love, mouths wide open like baby birds waiting for worms, or as defensive and hostile as the most surly teenager is capable of. But don't let outward appearances fool you—no matter who your stepchild is, he or she longs to be known and appreciated. And no matter what situation you find yourself in, make no mistake in recognizing that your stepchild is as least as angry and scared as you—and with less experience in dealing with such strong feelings.

So there they are in front of you, with at *least* the intensity of emotions you are experiencing. They have not been on the Earth very long and have been through a lot already—the divorce or death of a parent; maybe several "potential stepparents" when Mom or Dad was dating; perhaps even a stepparent or two already. If we are willing to feel compassion toward these young souls, our hearts will naturally open as we empathetically relate to the suffering they have already gone through, the confusion they must be feeling right now. And when our hearts are open, our love will flow more freely—regardless of their ability to receive it in the moment.

# GIVE UP YOUR DREAM OF
# THE PERFECT FAMILY

Do you have an image of the perfect family? Chances are it comes from television. Depending on your age, it might be the Cleavers from *Leave It to Beaver*, the Keatons from *Family Ties*, or the Huxtables from *Cosby*. No matter which, these were all "intact" families with parents who loved each other well and communicated perfectly, and kids who, despite minor squabbles, got along heartwarmingly with one another and ultimately always took their parents' advice. These paragon families always celebrated Christmas and birthdays together, and went on happy family vacations.

In shape and substance, these media families probably bear little resemblance to the kind of family structure you now find yourself in. This can be hard. When we set ourselves up for a particular circumstance and it doesn't come to pass, we can get so focused on what we don't have that we can fail to appreciate what we do have. In particular, the nuclear family is a very potent archetype, which means it is locked into our deep unconscious as a model of how family life should be. When in reality we experience something different, there can be profound sadness or anger.

Rachel remembers how hard it was for her to come to terms with remembers. "I couldn't stand thinking of myself that way so that I kept pretending it wasn't true. But the more I pretended, the more angry and upset I got at myself, Bill, and his kids. It was only when I finally admitted to myself that I had negative feelings that I could begin to resolve them."

Take two minutes to make contact with reality: How do you feel about your role as a stepparent? About your stepkids, your spouse? Your living arrangements? And then comes the most important part—just sit with what is. Recognize the emotional truth of your situation—Oh, I'm hurt at getting no positive reinforcement from my stepchildren despite all I do for them; I'm angry at my wife's ex for not ponying up his share of the child support—and then hold it in the spaciousness of your consciousness for a quiet few minutes and go about your day. The next day, check in again with yourself—Yup, I'm still angry; I'm a bit less hurt cause Zoe smiled at me today—whatever's true for you.

This practice is about you accepting what is, not you blasting your ex or the kids or husband with what you've discovered. Maybe some day it will be appropriate to share—in loving language—some insight you've gained, but for the most part, the daily check-in is about you coming into the present moment. If you persist over time, chances are you will see how much your feelings, and the situation, change. Sometimes for the worse, but more likely, for the better, if only because your capacity to accept the way things are will have increased tenfold.

# BE REALISTIC ABOUT YOUR ROLE

We ask a lot of kids when we create blended families. No matter how old or young the child is, they already have a mother and a father, whom, for the most part, they still wish would live together. Then one (or both) parent asks that the child accept into their lives another parent (or two or three—we know several people who have had three stepmothers). The situation is not the child's doing; they have no choice in the matter. They must simply accept a new stepmother or father. No wonder they often create havoc for us.

The truth, of course, is that the child already has a mother and a father (even if the parents are dead or gone), and we can never fill that role, no matter how much we may care or try to. And no matter how much we try, they may never love us the way we would like to be loved. (Which doesn't mean we have to put up with bad behavior; they must treat us decently, as we would have them treat any other human being, no matter how they feel.)

Every single stepparent we spoke to for this book, no matter their circumstances, said the same thing—as long as they tried to be their stepchild's mother or father, and expected the love the "real" mother or father would receive, they were disappointed. But if they were willing to give up that particular parental role and listen for what the child really needed from them, they were able to forge a relationship that worked. And sometimes, it can develop into something as precious as parenthood.

"Bonnie's kids Lisa and Tim were eight and six when I came on the scene," remembers Tom. "Their father had abandoned Bonnie, but they were still resistant to my becoming their father. So I suggested they call me by my first name, which made them both a bit more comfortable. I kept my emotional distance, but became the all-around homework helper, and gradually I saw their respect and love grow. In high school, they both made contact with their father, but when it came time for Lisa to get married, while her father was there, it was me she wanted to have escort her down the aisle."

By not forcing our stepchildren to love us or see us as mother or father, we give them the emotional space they need to find their way to us.

# CREATE AN IDENTITY
# FOR YOURSELF

So if you can't take on the role of parent, who should you be? That is a question that only you can answer, depending on your personality, circumstances, the ages and personalities of your stepkids, and so on. But we do encourage you to create an identity for yourself and make it explicit to the kids. Humor really helps here.

Judy's life-partner Will always signed cards, notes, and presents to Judy's daughter Amanda: "From the man who ruined your childhood," which is what she claimed he had done. Sometimes she would scream, "I hate you! I hate you!" A couple hours or days later when the conflict had been long forgotten or resolved, Will would joke and laugh with Amanda, referring to himself as "the man you love to hate."

Through such humor, we tell our stepkids that we *are* in their lives, and that while we know they might not always be happy about that, we are an adult they must come to terms with. We also show that their feelings are not deadly, that it hasn't killed us that they said such a thing. This is important because children can get swamped by the strength of their feelings and believe they, as children, are omnipotent. When we make light of such remarks, they can see our sturdiness and rest in our strength.

Bridging the identity gap between how the children view you and how you'd like to be seen starts by receiving unpleasant news without freaking out. When Todd told his stepmom, "I don't like you," she kindly responded with, "You don't have to like me, if you choose not to, but I'm trying to like you." Peter told stepdaughter Amy, "I'm glad you can voice your negative feelings about me." By allowing her to do so, eventually she felt safe enough with him to share her anger toward her dad, with whom she didn't dare share her deep thoughts and feelings for fear he would abandon her completely.

Perhaps in the beginning your identity to the kids is that of an unwelcome intruder, but if you can be good-natured about it all, it can change from being an outsider to observer to being a sounding board and confidante. It depends on you. No one can step into a family and become an instant parent. If you can remember that your identity doesn't depend on what the kids call you or how they treat you, but rather on how you behave toward them, you'll be on the right track.

# MAKE PEACE WITH MINE VERSUS YOURS

Melanie raised seven children: three stepsons, two sons from her first marriage, and two children with her second husband. "Our house was a revolving door," she says. "We were the full spectrum: steps, halfs, and fulls, but we never referred to anyone as 'yours' or mine. They were all ours." When talking about one to the other it was, 'He's your brother, she's your sister.'

"We tried to keep the rules the same even if our sons were only with us part time, but it didn't always work out. Sometimes I thought my husband was too easy on his kids, other times he was convinced I was too hard on his and more lenient with mine. Then there were times when I was harder on mine and let his squeeze by."

While some experts might advise you to get over the "yours versus mine" attitude, don't worry if you can't get there. It may not be humanly possible. Your kids will always be yours; his kids will always be his. You bring to your union years of personal history which can't be wiped out so quickly. It's natural to have a unique love for your own child. Kids sense this and can cope with it better if you're honest about your tendencies.

Acknowledging that each parent prefers his or her own child is healthier than sweeping it under the rug. No need to get flustered, defensive, or contrary. The kids will respect your integrity and together you can finds ways to make up for the discrepancies. Admitting the inconsistencies works better than being hypervigilant to make sure every interaction is equal.

It also affects how stepsiblings get along. Joel brought his eight-year-old daughter, Molly, his bride Alyce, and ten-year-old step-daughter, Amelia, to counseling. Everything had been going smoothly until the wedding, when Molly suddenly withdrew, becoming more tearful and sullen each day. Joel was at a loss as to why things had changed. As Judy talked with them, Molly became more and more agitated and burst out, "I hate Amelia because my dad likes her just the same as me." It turns out that Joel had told the girls on the eve of the wedding, "From now on you're my girls—I love you the same." Molly was devastated, wondering how her father could love Amelia, whom he'd only know for a year, as much as he loved her.

Children need to know that they cannot be replaced so quickly in their parents' hearts. When you demote your child from the number-one position he once held, he feels emotionally abandoned, but when you tell him: "You're always number one in my heart," he can cope more easily with sharing you. Letting your child know that you will always love her and be there for her, above all else, can make a huge difference in your child's acceptance of stepsiblings.

# UNDERSTAND YOU'RE THE ADULT

Boy, is *this* a challenge. No matter what your parental status—parent or stepparent—there are times when all you want to do is to give in to the urge to scream, cry, hit, or throw yourself down on the ground like a two-year-old, pounding and kicking the floor.

And because of the complexities of stepparenting, the urge might strike quite a lot. Like when four-year-old Johnny, who is visiting for two months of summer vacation, screams at the top of his lungs in the store, "You're not my mom. I don't have to do what you say!" or Shelby announces in the middle of a business dinner party for twelve, "I hate you and wish you were dead." Or seven-year-old Samantha, in a fit of pique over your not allowing her to pierce her ears, threatens to move in permanently with her father and never show her face at your house again.

It's hard to resist walking out on Johnny in the store or saying "I hate you too, Shelby," or "Good, I'll be glad to get rid of you, Samantha," isn't it? Deep inside we have little selves the same age as Johnny and Shelby and Samantha and they have just gotten their feelings hurt. But one of the soul challenges that stepparenting continually calls us to face is to remember that we are now adults and as such have a responsibility to act more maturely than the beings in front of us. When we agreed to create this new family we took on an obligation to bring all our maturity to bear upon the situation and always to try to act for the highest good of the young ones in our care. This doesn't mean we will always succeed. We will lose our tempers and our tongues on occasion (for which we will later apologize). But in the heat of the moment, it's important to remember that the child in front of us who is acting so badly is at least as angry and hurt as we are (why else would they be saying such things?) and it is our job to figure out what he or she really needs.

Whatever situation you and your stepchildren are in—living together part-time, living together full-time and never seeing their other parent, visiting only on weekends or summer vacation, whatever—always remember that as tough as it is for you, it is that much harder for them. As children, they have fewer emotional resources and less control over the arrangements of their lives. If you remember that you are an adult and they are only children, it will make whatever negativity they fling in your direction easier to bear.

# FIND A SAFE HAVEN TO VENT

No matter how wonderful your family situation is, some times will be hard, horrible, even hellish, so be sure to have at least one friend who will listen sympathetically, offer support, and remind you of the worth of what you are doing.

"I've been fortunate to have a friend who started on the step-mother journey exactly at the same time as I did," says Anna. "She was the stepmother of three children who lived with her full-time, and I had two half-time. Neither of us had children of our own. We would talk frequently and at least once a year, we'd go away for a weekend of bitching, moaning, and complaining. It was great to discover that virtually everything I was experiencing she was also feeling. We would talk about feeling the pain of the undefined role—being ignored at high school graduation in favor of the 'real' parents, for example; our anger at the lack of privacy and intimacy with our spouse; our resentment over our increased workload—laundry and meals and car pools without receiving the kind of love the kids showered on their biological parents; and the financial strain and obligation we were forced to meet because of 'their' children. All the things we couldn't discuss with our mates because it would be too hurtful or with our other friends because they couldn't understand.

"We would commiserate with one another—it felt so good to be so totally understood—and somehow knowing that we weren't alone in feeling the way we did made it so much easier to keep on going."

Do you have someone you can pour out your heart to? It needs to be someone other than your mate. As loving and understanding as he or she might be, no one wants to hear what a drag their children are, and not many relationships can stand the burden of the kind of resentments that you might want to vent in the heat of the moment. Ideally, it would be another stepparent. If you don't have a good friend, consider joining a group or a stepparent chat room on the Internet. They should be easy to locate. But no matter where you look, be sure to find a sympathetic ear or two.

# BE READY FOR TOUGH QUESTIONS

"I will remember this day as long as I live," says Anna. "I was twenty-five years old, and suddenly found myself the stepmother of Michael, age two, and Zoe, age six months, who lived half the week with us and half the week with their mother. It was about six months into the creation of our new household, and we were sitting around eating dinner when three-year-old Michael looked straight at me (he had mostly ignored me to that point) and said, 'Why won't you let my dad come home?'

"I was stunned into silence as the enormity of the question and all its implications reverberated around me. How could I possibly explain to a three-year-old the complexities of adult emotional life? How could I deal with the fact that his mother had obviously blamed me for the situation and now he did too (not to mention that his remark revealed that 'home' to him was the other house, not where we lived)? I turned to his father for help; I can't remember what he said in response.

"I know I said nothing and even now, twenty years later, I regret that. If only someone had taken me aside beforehand and said, 'This is going to be hard. It's going to be hard on you and even harder on the kids. Be ready for tough questions. If you don't know what to say, tell them their question matters to you and you are going to think about it. Then get advice—from a therapist, an experienced friend, a book.'"

And so now, this is our advice to you—be prepared for the unexpected: the tough question, the difficult situation. By being emotionally prepared, you can gather the resources you need when the time comes.

# ACKNOWLEDGE YOUR
# FEELINGS OF JEALOUSY

I spent years resenting the amount of time my husband spent with his kids, and they resented the time he spent with me, I discovered recently from my stepdaughter," says Marie, a stepmother of two children. "For several years they lived three hundred miles away and Don would drive down to see them for the weekend at least once a month. I was lonely and blamed the kids for my situation. Even when I would go or they would come to our house, I felt as though I was irrelevant. They had a mom and a dad and were not interested in a relationship with me. Even though they didn't live with us full-time, I felt like the three of them were a family and I was an outsider. Perhaps if I had had a child of my own the feeling would not have been so strong."

Fred, on the other hand, was extremely jealous of Cynthia's previous husband, Walter. Her kids were a constant reminder that she had loved another man, and because they shared custody, Cynthia saw Walter frequently, which drove Fred up the wall.

Many times in divorce situations, stepparents feel jealous—of the ex-spouse, the time and attention the children get, the money that gets spent on the stepkids, the fact that the spouse has children and you do not. In stepfamilies, there are a myriad of ways to feel jealous and excluded. Again, the trick is first to acknowledge the truth of how you feel: for example, "Yes, I am jealous every time Don goes over to Sue's house to get the kids." Sit with the truth of how you feel without judgment, without trying to fix it or change it—"Yup, there it is, jealousy again. Yup."

By sitting quietly with it, the feeling may begin to shift. If it doesn't, you might want to find a time to talk over the issue with your mate. Choose a good time (not when he's got one foot out the door to Sue's house!) and quietly verbalize your feelings. Perhaps verbalizing them and hearing his or her assurances is all you need. Or maybe together you can come up with a solution that can accommodate everyone: Don will ask the kids to meet him in the front yard, for instance.

The trick is to acknowledge your true feelings, discover whether something has to be done about them and then present the situation in as nonconfrontational a manner as possible. (And go easy on yourself if you don't do this perfectly—it's hard!)

# DON'T EXPECT TO BE
# THANKED OVERTLY

There's an old saying that parenting is a thankless task, but it's an understatement where stepparenting is concerned. After all, especially when they are little, kids are generally loving and sweet toward their parents—kissing, hugging, bringing them pictures and presents they made in school. But with stepparents, it's the third-wheel problem again. You are often perceived to be an extraneous or even unwanted addition. And the stepchildren might feel very disloyal about showing you appreciation or affection, particularly if the ex has vilified you. No wonder they don't thank you for being in their lives.

"I was highly sensitive to this issue," says Francine, a mother of two and stepmother of two. "Every Mother's Day, my kids made me cards, but there was never anything from my stepkids. I felt unrecognized and unappreciated for all the work I do—cooking, cleaning, shlepping. . . . I started to dread the day. It reminded me that my stepkids never say 'I love you' to me either and that hurts a lot too."

There are no easy answers to such hurt. But one possible balm is to give up any expectations (expectations *always* cause angst because no one can live up to anyone else's), but live with expectancy—which is an openness to something positive happening. Francine hasn't gotten a Mother's Day card yet, but three years into her role as a stepmother, her stepdaughter Kate said to her one day, "I love the way you make chocolate chip cookies and put a special message inside my lunch bag. All the other kids at school are jealous." Because she kept her heart open and offered loving care to her stepchildren without expecting gratitude, she received the thanks she so richly deserved.

# ALWAYS REMEMBER YOUR STEPCHILDREN LOVE THEIR OTHER PARENT

Depending on your circumstances, this may take emotional and spiritual maturity. "Bill had the ex-wife from hell, and she had her guns trained on me," remembers Anna. "She blamed me for the divorce and acted out in all kinds of ways—she broke into our house and destroyed my clothes, she called hundreds of times a day and hung on the phone not speaking. Every time Bill went to drop off the kids after the weekend, they fought. We finally had to get an unlisted phone number and designate a friend as the number she could call in case of emergency, and enlisted mutual friends to be the go-betweens for kid transfers. Even after years passed and tempers cooled somewhat, she refused to ever be in the same room with me and still has never spoken to me.

"Nonetheless, the kids never heard a bad word pass my lips about their mother. I vowed to myself that I would never put them in the position of feeling disloyal to her or feeling guilty about loving her. Whenever something painful to me would come up—that I was banned from eighth-grade graduation or the tennis tournament, say—rather than exploding, I would try and remember that their mother was a soul just as I was, trying the best she could, and that it was her woundedness that was causing her to act the way she did. She never knew me; my attempts at understanding and acceptance were all private. But I know in my heart that my stepkids, spouse, and I all benefited from my silently sending love rather than hate, peace rather than enmity."

As Joyce and Barry Vissell say in their wonderful book *Models of Love*, "On some level children must all feel that they are a deep part of both their mother and their father. When a mother [or stepmother] complains to her son about his father, the child feels she is also attacking him. In their childlike simplicity they reason, 'You think my daddy is no good. Since I'm a part of daddy, you must feel I am no good too.'" Don't play bash the ex; let your stepkids have their loving feelings unconflictedly.

# GET A DIPLOMA IN DIPLOMACY

Do we stepparents need this one! We need it when our stepkids are waxing eloquently about their "real" father, whom we know is a drunk who abused them and their mother, or when they tell us all about their wonderful mother, whom we know to be a narcissistic hysteric who couldn't love a child if you gave her a million dollars to do it. We have to remember that these are our stepchildren's parents, and it is not our job to disillusion them (most likely they will see the truth as young adults on their own; coming to terms with their parents is a job only they can do). If you're tempted to try, it's helpful to remember that all that is likely to happen is that they will end up hating *you* for badmouthing their beloved.

So what do you say that is honest and not hurtful? "This is where the diplomacy degree comes in," says Anna. "What I used to say was something simple like, 'I'm glad you love your mother.' Or 'It's great that you have so many people who love you.' That way I neither affirmed nor disagreed with what they were saying, but responded to the emotional need I thought they were expressing."

The diplomacy degree comes in handy almost daily: when seven-year-old Chloe shows up from her mother's with makeup on and mother's approval; when fourteen-year-old Josh brings the "cool gun" his father bought him into your pacifist household. You have to negotiate these tricky waters without denigrating the other parent, for the more you rail against the bad judgment, character, or habits of the ex-spouse, the more you drive your stepchild away from you and into the other parent's arms.

This is particularly tricky if the other person is dead. We have a friend who married a widower with three kids. "Try competing with a dead mother," bemoans Shirley. "She has become a saint in their minds because she is no longer around to disappoint and fail them as all parents do. Everything I do is compared to the fantasized behavior of this paragon of love."

No matter what your situation, badmouthing the ex is the quickest way to disaster. You don't have to like her, you don't have to let the gun he gave Josh into your house, but if you want a happy relationship with your stepchildren, you do have to figure out how to speak pleasantly of their other parent.

# LIGHTEN UP

Recently we read a Miss Manners column in which a single parent described being hurt by her fiancé's child's comment. On the way to a video arcade with both sets of kids, Junior piped up with something like, "I wish it were just you and me, Dad, and nobody else going to play." The writer was expressing hurt and anger that her fiancé did nothing to "correct" Junior's behavior.

If this woman was upset enough to write to Miss Manners about Junior, she is in for a rough ride as a stepmother! Of course Junior said it on purpose to hurt her feelings and will continue to say such things (and much worse!) if he gets the reaction he wants—which is to create distance, division, and discord so that (he hopes) she and her kids will go away.

In such circumstances, what works best is to lighten up and not take such comments too seriously. A simple lighthearted, "Oh yes, it's nice to do things alone with your father sometimes, but today we're all playing together" would have sufficed. If you can think of a witty repartee, that is even better. Or ignore the comment altogether and challenge him to a one-on-one game of Mario Cart or Double 007 Golden Eye.

If you have children of your own who are also being snubbed, be sure to talk to them privately about the situation later: "Did Junior hurt your feelings? He's mad about sharing time with his dad. It's not personal."

Treat such "barbs" lightly and they will diminish over time. Take them too seriously and you will spend a great deal of time being hurt.

# GO EASY ON YOURSELF

Stepparenting is tricky business and you are not always going to do it right. So while you are being understanding and tolerant toward the difficulties your stepchildren face, be sure to give yourself the same amount of compassion. You will say or do the wrong thing sometimes. You will have negative thoughts toward your mate and stepkids. As long as you sincerely apologize for anything you verbalize, you don't need to wallow in guilt. In fact, it is counterproductive.

"For the longest time I used to feel guilty because I didn't love my stepkids the way my husband did," recalls Anna. "I hated myself for not loving them, I hated them because their presence was a constant reminder of my lack of loving feelings, and I hated my husband for 'getting' me into the mess in the first place. As long as I expected to have the same warm and fuzzy feelings as Bill did, I could not be open to the positive feelings I did experience toward them. When I stopped 'shoulding,' I began to go easier on myself and then was able to go easier on them. These days, as my stepdaughter reaches her late teens, she gets along much better with me than she does with her father, who 'loves' her more than I do."

We know lots of stepparents who love their stepkids, and virtually every one of them would admit that it is not exactly in the same way as a parent loves his or her child. That might not be all bad;

parental love can be so ego-involved that we try to get our kids to live out our unfulfilled dreams. As stepparents, we have less ego involvement and therefore perhaps more ability to see our stepchildren for the unique souls they are. As long as we hold their highest good foremost in our hearts as we interact with them, we will have done our job well.

So go easy on yourself when you feel frustrated, cranky, or unloving. You are doing the best you can and chances are that's very good indeed.

# CHERISH THE ABSURD

Let's be brutally honest here: Marrying someone doesn't automatically make you a parent. Oh yes, you act like a parent because of all the stuff you're doing. You might even be doing the job brilliantly but still you aren't entitled to the position until you've earned it. The privilege of being a parent to someone else's children is earned through considerable pain and sacrifice. Just as a woman gives birth following bouts of morning sickness, stretch marks, bloating, and excruciating labor pains, so too will you become a stepmother or a stepfather only after enduring substantial torture and testing. To be a parent you must first survive the initiation. And as you've found out by now there's plenty of hazing to endure. Don't take it personally; it's the path each stepparent walks.

Let's face it—you had no way of knowing when you married the "love of your life with the adorable little kids" what you were signing up for. Becoming a blended family is complex; after all, you're dealing with family history that you had no part in writing.

When two families come together there are bound to be competition and jealousy, rejection and anger. Each family is a multidimensional system with its own peculiar operating procedures, and there's mounds of confusion to climb over when you put them together. For example, Claire was dumbfounded when her surly ten-year-old stepson answered her request to take off his muddy shoes, "You're not my mother, you can't make me!" This was followed by, "Will you make us tacos for lunch?"

The more difficult your situation, the more you need laughter. Without a sense of the ridiculous and a well-developed appreciation of the absurd, the rough spots will split into caverns. According to the Stepfamily Association of America, it takes five to seven years for an expanded family with young stepchildren to reach some stability. If a teenager is involved, it may never happen.

As a stepparent, you'll have to develop the knack of stepping back, letting go, and observing the goings on around you. Make no mistake about it—while you're being ignored, you're being watched and tested. The harder you try to assume the role of new parent, the harder the children will resist; the less you try to take over, the better the chances for happiness. It's true, you can't become an instant parent, but while you're cooking the meals and doing the laundry you can finely tune your sense of the inane.

# GIVE YOURSELF CREDIT FOR A JOB WELL DONE

Do you focus on what you've done well as a stepparent, or do you only dwell on the negative? One way to make the experience as positive as possible is to do a little one-minute inventory at the end of the day (or whenever the kids are around): I like the way I handled the situation with Ben when he was so upset at himself for losing the tennis match; I did well on the phone with Martha's ex; John and I did well not to get pulled into our kids' fight with one another—for a change they actually worked it out well.

By focusing on the positive—we're doing a pretty good job—we give our psyches a boost, which makes it easier to keep on going. Noticing what's right also trains the brain to respond that way when a similar situation comes up again. It also allows our mind to think about ways to adapt what's working to other situations. When we focus on the negative, all we tell ourselves is that we don't know what we're doing and we get disheartened. Our creative thinking shuts down and our options of response dwindle. If all we notice is that we yelled, the next time all we will know how to do is yell—and then feel more guilty that we haven't stopped yelling.

So appreciate yourself today for all that you have done right as a stepparent! Get yourself a package of gold stars and award then to yourself. Tell a friend three things you're proud of as a stepparent today. Remember—It's not just "idle" praise. The more you focus on the positive, the more you will remember to do well in the future.

# KNOW YOU'RE NOT ALONE

For most stepparents, the process of being involved with someone else's children is not a walk in the park. Sometimes, when you are tempted to sink into despair and take the situation too personally, it really helps to remember that you are not alone in facing difficulties. In other words, it's not a personal failing on your part that is making stepparenting challenging or downright difficult—it just is hard, at least some of the time.

It's hard not to take an adolescent boy's silent animosity or a girl's acting out toward you personally—after all, they are persons who are directing their sullenness or open anger directly at you. But if you can remember that millions of people, both kids and adults, are struggling with the exact same issues, it can help you to depersonalize the situation a bit. From the distance that depersonalizing creates, you can perhaps regain your lightheartedness and good humor.

"I remember once when Michael was going through a particularly surly teenage phase and his father was working 'round the clock, and I was feeling resentful that I had to care for such a nasty and ungrateful stepchild," says Anna. "I went around in a huff for days, but finally decided that perhaps I could break the mood with a little humor. So the next day, when he was arguing with me over whether the sky was truly blue (honest!), I said with humor in my tone, 'I know it's your job as a teenager to disagree with whatever an adult says and particularly with me, but could you take a vacation from your job for the rest of the evening?' I can't say that he actually laughed, but he did lighten up and treated me well the rest of the day."

One excellent way to remember that you are not alone is to join a support group. It's great to have folks to commiserate with, and maybe other people will offer creative solutions to situations that have stalemated you. If you don't know of any existing groups, go ahead and make one of your own. We suggest you hold meetings away from prying ears and eyes so that you feel free to express your emotional truth. One word of caution—commiserating is one thing, but getting caught forever in a cycle of negativity toward exes and stepkids is another. Make a commitment in your group to focus on positive solutions and to help one another seek the good and avoid wallowing in bitterness and anger.

# REMEMBER YOU CHOSE THIS

When things get rough, it's important to remember that you chose this relationship in the first place. You fell in love with a person who had children, and you agreed to accept the children into the new family you are creating. You may secretly wish he didn't have kids; you may hope that she doesn't get custody, but the truth is when you get involved with a person with kids, you are taking on the new identity of stepparent even if at this moment the kids aren't on the scene. You can do it willingly or kicking and screaming, but *you are choosing to do it.*

"For the longest time, I saw myself as a person in love with Bill, a man who just *happened* to have two children who lived with him half-time," says Anna. "I glossed over the fact that his kids were a huge part of his life and in making a commitment to him, I had to make a commitment to his children as well. I didn't want it to be true, so I pretended it wasn't, even though the kids were there every Friday through Sunday.

"Finally I realized—I had *chosen* this situation. Even though I did not consciously choose, even though up till then I would have denied I chose, the fact was I had. It wasn't a 'coincidence' that Bill had kids. It was part of what I was signing up for. And it was perfect for me— I was able to parent without being 'the mother,' which, as the daughter of a very difficult alcoholic mother, was too scary for me. This way I could do it without having the full burden of the role."

Anna is friends with a couple who each had two kids, ages eight and ten. When the couple married, her kids lived with them and his kids lived with his ex-wife. Then his ex-wife was murdered, and suddenly they had four kids under one roof. It was difficult, to say the least. The kids were in open warfare with one another, and two were grieving the death of their mother. The couple could easily say that they had not chosen this particular situation.

True, but when they meet and decided to marry, they did know that there were four kids. And given the vagaries of life—death, changing custody arrangements particularly as children get older and express preferences—they knew somewhere in themselves that they were at least potentially taking on the responsibility of the whole brood. Unfortunately, this couple did not see their choice in the situation. As a consequence, they remained bitter and angry, and their children, now in their thirties, are all estranged from them and from one another.

We may have chosen consciously or unconsciously, but we have agreed to participate in this new configuration. If we can feel our choosing and look for the underlying positive reasons for our choice, it will make the day-to-day easier.

# SEARCH FOR THE SOUL GROWTH

Each and every one of us is here on Earth to grow our souls, to become the best of who we can be, love as well as we can, and offer our unique gifts to the world. To do these tasks well, we need to be constantly asking ourselves as we navigate the whitewater rapids of life: What is being asked of me here in terms of soul growth? Am I being called to be more forgiving? Less angry? More receptive? Less fearful?

All of life is a school for the soul, a series of "classes" in which we are called upon to learn the lessons and move to the next level. Seen in this light, all of our challenges—whether they have to do with our health, relationships, or work—are opportunities to grow our souls bigger and wider and to live more fully and deeply. In this sense, those of us who are stepparents have been given the special opportunity to grow our souls through the experience of interacting with and helping to *care for and guide* someone else's children.

To live with this awareness at the forefront of our minds is to change dramatically our relationship to the challenges of stepparenting. Rather than dwelling on the negatives—I can't get any respect, the ex-wife is driving me insane, the kids are wild when they come back from a weekend with Dad—this perspective asks us to discover what each challenge is calling for in terms of our soul development.

Is it more tolerance? Less selfishness? More compassion or patience? A willingness to let go of a grudge?

Ellen, whose parents were killed when she was eight years old, grew up being shuffled from one relative to another. An only child, lonely and isolated, she escaped into books and her studies. Secretly she longed for brothers and sisters and prayed every day that she would some day have a family. In her mid-thirties, she fell in love with and married David, a widower with three small children. She knew this family was the answer to her prayers, and she happily gave up her career to become a wife and a mother.

Thus began the difficult task of healing. When seven-year-old Lindsey cried, "I want my mommy in heaven, not you," Ellen was shaken to her soul. She hadn't cried when her own mother died twenty-nine years before, and she didn't know how to comfort Lindsey. For months, she withdrew into books and thought about leaving, but fortunately she didn't. If she was to discover her soul lessons, this was indeed the perfect family in which to do it.

No matter what the particulars of your situation, you are enrolled in stepparenting school and the object of the learning is to become the most loving, wise, compassionate self that you are capable of being. To be willing always to look for the lesson is to imbue your role with the highest mission and receive from it the highest reward.

# DEALING WITH YOUR SPOUSE

*The meeting of two persons'
abilities is like the contact of two
chemical substances: if there is any
reaction, both are transformed.*

—Carl Jung

# TALK, TALK, TALK
# TO YOUR PARTNER

Good communication is a hallmark of any healthy relationship, and nowhere is it more necessary than between the adults who live in a family with stepchildren. Probably you did a tremendous amount of talking *before* you made the commitment to live together, and you have some mutually agreed-upon principles regarding the children in your life. But love is often blind, even the second or third time around, so perhaps you didn't fully explore the kinds of issues you are now facing. In either case, life has a way of throwing curveballs at us, so that chances are even if you did discuss parenting, you are encountering situations you never dreamed possible.

That's why it's so important to keep on talking to one another about what is going on—how you both are feeling, what you think the kids might be needing, how to handle the request for a change in the custody arrangements. And be sure to do it in private, so that the kids are protected from your uncensored remarks. ("One of the advantages of joint custody," notes Anna, "is it gives you time alone. Of course you end up using a lot of it talking about the kids.")

Be very careful about how you communicate your negative feelings or impressions to your mate. Remember he or she loves their child very much and might get defensive if you appear to be on the attack. If you, with a more objective eye, see something that needs addressing, be sure to choose the time and your words carefully or your comments could backfire on you.

"When Bill and I first started living together, he felt very guilty about the divorce's effect on his three-year-old son Michael. So he was hesitant to discipline him at all and Michael was running wild. I hung back for a few weeks, waiting to see what would happen and feeling it was not my place, at least not yet, to discipline Michael. Finally I said something to Bill. He admitted that his guilt was holding him back from doing the right thing. Then he said that he was going to take Michael on a week's vacation alone, so that Michael could feel Bill's love and receive some undivided attention. When they returned, he would be willing to start enforcing the rules. Well, Bill stuck to his word and we had a few rocky days as Michael rebelled against the new regime. I know that if I had said something sooner, Bill would not have been ready to hear me."

Sometimes feelings get so volatile that good communication between you is not possible. If you find yourself in that place, please seek out professional help—a minister, a therapist. He or she can help you find a bridge back to one another.

# BREAK THE MOLD AND
# DESIGN A NEW MODEL

If you only remember one thing about the process of becoming a blended family, remember this: You can't instantly take over the parenting functions for children who are not your own. When Judy sees blended families in her family counseling practice, she asks the children what kind of relationship they would like to have with their parent's new wife or husband. "In all the years I've been asking this question I have never had a child answer, 'I'd like her to be a mother to me,' or 'I'd like him to be another father.'"

Children are not looking for another parent—even if one of their parents has died. What they do wish for is a friendly relationship. They'd like the new spouse to be like a special coach or helpful teacher, a confidante, a grown-up buddy, a mentor. They want their parents to treat all the children and each other well. They wish for harmony, courtesy, and respect between *all* the adults, including exes.

The blended families Judy has worked with who have been able to accomplish a harmonious family life have done so by first breaking out of the stereotypical mold of what a stepmother or stepfather is suppose to be and do, and have started from scratch. Instead of trying to look like a traditional nuclear family, they have carved out a new model for their expanded family.

To create a harmonious blended family, you don't have to function like the nuclear family you grew up in. In a blended family it works best if the biological parent continues to be responsible for the parenting of his or her own children. Traditionally, when Dad remarries, bringing children to the new household, he turns the parenting over to Stepmom, then more or less withdraws. This old model keeps the new spouse locked in the "wicked stepmother" position. Instead of living on the outskirts of family life, the biological parent must stay active in all aspects of parenting and family life. When the biological parent steps up to his or her parenting obligations, the new spouse gets the luxury of relaxed time with the children, and their relationship develops in a more satisfying direction.

Tim has custody of his three children, ages seven, nine, and ten. When Sarah, his fiancée, moved in and assumed the role of mother, family life deteriorated rapidly. In desperation, they came to counseling and constructed a model for their family that had greater potential for success. The first change made was that Sarah relinquished the mother role and went to work full-time. Tim cut his overtime work hours and took back the "mother and father" role he had assumed for the previous three years. Sarah once again could relate to the kids as the family friend. Everyone was happier and the wedding date was set. Now, after three years of marriage, the kids call her "Our Sarah."

# BE GOOD HOUSEMATES

Here's a bit of advice from Elizabeth, who lives with her husband Don and four teenage stepsons: "Don't get caught up on the word *family*. Family is a concept with so much emotional charge behind it that trying to turn your household into one can bog you down with unruly expectations."

"We call ourselves 'five bachelors and a babe,'" said Don, who recognized early on that his boys, whom he had raised for six years by himself, were not about to accept Elizabeth as mother. "I didn't have a clue how to live with spirited testosterone-charged young men," said Elizabeth, "so instead of mothering them we work on becoming good housemates." Don agrees, "In many ways we're closer than most families I see, yet that's not how we describe ourselves."

Whether you call yourself a tribe, a clan, kindred souls, housemates, or enemies living under one roof, it doesn't matter as much as your attitude. With a little imagination, you can come up with a title that describes your state of affairs in a fresh and lively way.

Begin by brainstorming a description or title for your group. Think of your living situation as a television sitcom—what title can you give it that would draw the largest audience? Think of a title that will make the other members of the group sit up and take notice. In a stepparenting class, one family decided to call themselves, "The Brady

Bunch Goes to War"; another called themselves, "The Mighty Six."

By thinking of yourself as housemates you remove the authoritarian edge and move more easily into collaboration. "We've ground out housemate policies for everything from where to keep the boys' cereal to 'hands off' signs on my private shelf in the cupboard," says Elizabeth. "They teach me 'guy stuff' like how to ride dirt bikes and spit; I teach them to take their shoes off in the house, and to appreciate flowers and candles, and other 'girlie' stuff."

In describing your living arrangements and in making housemate policies, begin where you are, not where you think you should be. If you're joining forces, for example, with a bunch of boys who have never sat a table for dinner, you can't expect to have formal dining off the bat. Begin by making a proposal to eat around a table one night a week. Enlist their cooperation by pleading, bribing, and begging if you must—but no nagging or threatening.

Keep the discussions on household policies lively by joking, being silly, and exaggerating the obvious. "Okay, let's live as dirty slobs for one week," said one stepmother, while trying to establish household procedures for the laundry room. When you think of your group as a sitcom and your housemates as cast members you take the pressure off. There's no need to create a happily-ever-after ending. All you need is for each episode to be entertaining.

# MERGE YOUR PARENTING STYLES

The best thing about Bill's and my parenting styles," recalls Anna, "is that we almost never disagreed. We really had very similar philosophies that, moment to moment, translated into a style in which it was very easy to back one another up. So I was never pitted against the kids and Bill. In a disagreement, we stood together." But what if the two of you don't have a natural stylistic affinity or, as can happen, you believe your spouse is just plain wrong sometimes?

Kids sense when parents have different styles; they know who is the more lenient, for example, and who is stricter. And they will use that knowledge if you don't figure out a way to create at least a smidgen of unity. "Yes, Dad wants you to do the dishes immediately following dinner. So right now, please do it his way. Let's talk it over with him later and perhaps tomorrow we can try another way." Talking about your parenting differences in this way builds on your relationship with the kids while teaching respect for the other parent's ways. It shows them that you can work together even though you have differences.

Merge your styles by trying out each other's ways, and enlist the kids to participate in the process. Dad thinks we should do it this way, Mom thinks this way might work better. Ask the kids if they have a compromise. The Bensons were a blended family with some kids living with them full-time and others coming for weekends and extended holidays. One side of the family was easygoing about household habits and rules; the other side were clean fanatics and preferred a firm set of operating procedures. The complicated merger was achieved by enlisting everyone's input. The kids surprisingly came up with the solution: three slogans—"Cleanliness is harder, but better," "Treat each other respectfully," and "Negotiate the rest"—became their working philosophy. Involving the kids in the solutions places the emphasis on teamwork and cooperation rather than pitting parents against kids.

If your children are able to come between you to divide and conquer, you and your spouse may have unresolved parenting issues. If this is happening, you may need to write down a list of house rules that you both can agree to: bedtime at 8:00; no sweets till after dinner. When you are in agreement, you will be able to back each other up without giving mixed messages to the kids. The time you spend talking this over with each other will also help you find your merged parenting style.

So many kids of divorce have to deal with different rules at Mom's and Dad's. If the two of you are in harmony, that makes at least one place of solid ground for the kids to stand on.

# DEAL WITH DISCIPLINE

Nowhere is a merger of parenting philosophy more vital than in the area of discipline. What we mean here is that you and your spouse have to be in agreement with what is worth holding the line for, and how you are going to do it. Are the two of you going to enforce the rules with the kids, or are you as the stepparent going to hold back and let the biological parent take the lead?

No one can tell the two of you what to do or exactly how to do it, for particularly in blended families, it all depends on the circumstances. If you are parenting very young children who spend a great deal of time with you, it is probably best if you both establish yourselves as authority figures. But if you are a newcomer to the scene encountering a surly twelve-year-old whom you see only for a week at Christmas vacation, you might want to take a different tack than head-to-head confrontation to establish your authority.

In either case, you and your spouse need to talk about discipline and consequences—at best before the kids arrive, but if not, as soon after as possible. What are your ground rules? How have you dealt with disobedience in the past? How comfortable are your stepkids with you? How do you feel about your spouse telling your children what to do? These are all considerations in establishing the whats and hows of discipline.

So many stepparents disapprove of the way their spouse handles his or her children but are afraid to say anything. Unless the two of you can agree on a strategy—even if the strategy is that you, the stepparent, will stay out of it—there will be discord between you, and that will spill over into your lives with the kids. A discipline strategy that you both agree upon—a time-out for the offending child with conversation afterward to discuss the misbehavior, enforced by whoever was witness to the event, for example—will go a long way toward creating harmony at least between the two of you. When you believe that you will stand together and support the strategy you have created, you feel a strong, loving connection to your spouse, even when the kids are misbehaving. But if you don't have that unity, find yourselves fighting between yourselves, as well as with the children in your care.

# RIDE OUT THE
# COMPLEXITIES TOGETHER

"This one took me a long time to learn," remembers Anna. "When things got tough, I used to set Bill up as the villain, throwing things in his face like 'These are your ex-wife and your kids and it's all your fault that we are in this awful situation!' He would always say, 'I'm not the enemy. I'm on your side, trying to figure out the best thing to do for all of us.' I desperately wanted to blame someone, and he was the most convenient target. Needless to say, it was very destructive to our relationship. Even now, if things get really heated with one of the kids, I still have that tendency. But I've learned to try and breathe quietly and say to myself over and over, 'He's not the enemy. We can work this out together.'"

Blaming is a wonderfully easy relationship sinkhole, and it's particularly common for stepfamilies to fall into it. After all, at any given moment, it's the other person's kids (or ex) causing a ruckus. Why shouldn't he or she pay by being on the receiving end of our totally righteous anger?

Unless you want to end up in divorce court (again), avoid the blame sinkhole at all costs. Regardless of whose kids they are legally, by virtue of you and your spouse's commitment to one another, you are in this together, and together you need to find the way out.

This togetherness extends to all aspects of your lives. Whether it is simply trying to figure out the arrangements for getting two kids to soccer practice and one to piano lessons after school or negotiating a delicate peace between two children who are less than happy about being "blended," you need both your energies, commitment, and cooperation. If you want your relationship to thrive, there can be no room for "That's your problem because it's your kid," or "You deal with it because you created the mess in the first place." Come together and you won't have to come apart.

# LAUGH TOGETHER (A LOT)

Isn't laughter great? Laughter dispels tension, defuses anger, dilutes hostility. It's particularly wonderful for creating intimacy in a relationship, a private space between you and your mate where you acknowledge the humor in whatever is going on. Laughter bonds you together, which is particularly handy when the situation is threatening to tear you apart.

"I will never forget the day we had sent four-year-old Zoe to her room for a time-out," says Anna. "She was screaming and crying, 'I want my mom,' which she routinely did whenever Bill or I disciplined her. That always set my nerves on edge—I felt guilty about the situation and angry that she would hurt me by throwing her mother in my face. She wailed for a long time. Then we noticed there were longer and longer intervals between the wails, and they were losing intensity: Waah! Waah. Silence. Silence. Silence. *Waah.... Waah.* We snuck up to her room and peeked in the doorway. There she was, happily coloring away, until she would remember that she was supposed to be upset and let out a couple wails for our benefit. We snuck back downstairs and laughed together until our sides ached. We still laugh about it—sixteen years later."

Will asked seven-year-old Amanda how she would like to introduce him. She shrugged her shoulders, seemingly not to care. Will continued with the line of questioning, listing a number of options: "How about as your mother's friend, as your uncle, a family acquaintance, Mom's boyfriend, neighbor, stepdad?" Amanda continued ignoring him. Finally Will asked again, "How do you want to introduce me when your friends come over?" Amanda quietly answered, "As my mom's ex-boyfriend!" "We roared until tears were streaming down our cheeks." For the next seven years of Will's life, whenever Judy and Will had a tiff they'd tease each other and say, "Watch out or I'll introduce you as my ex."

Practice laughing with each other and smiling. At the end of the day, when you are alone, share a story about the funny things the kids said or did. Laugh about the insanity of it all. Your spouse will appreciate you so much if you can get into the habit of seeing the funny side of your situation. Laughter is the aphrodisiac your relationship needs to withstand the pulls that stepparenting will inevitably bring.

# ACKNOWLEDGE
# YOUR BOUNDARIES

Everyone, no matter how spiritually and emotionally mature, has limits. In fact, boundaries are healthy—when they serve to protect us from harm and do not limit our soul growth. When dealing with stepkids, it's important to acknowledge to your partner—in a loving way of course—where your limits are.

"Because of the rough start with Bill's ex-wife," says Anna, "I became very fearful of her. I was afraid of her anger toward me, and of her anger toward the kids as a consequence of their relationship with me. So one of my boundaries was that I would not do the kid transfers. No matter how hard I tried, I was just too afraid of her volatility to even consider it. It was a relief when the kids got old enough to take public transportation and could go back and forth on their own. I wish I could have come to the place where I could let go of my fear, but I never have."

There's a big difference between acknowledging boundaries and refusing to participate because "they're your kids." The first is a sincere, heartfelt acknowledgment that some of what needs to be done is just not possible for you to do right now. The other is an angry, resentful refusal to participate in the process. The first invites closeness; the second is a slap in the face.

Only you can know where your boundaries are, and only your spouse can report in on her or his own limits. Are there areas in your life where you feel put upon? Chores or activities that you feel resentful about doing? Make a list of things you don't like doing. Don't leave anything out. Put your list aside for a day or two and then read it over, placing a star by the three most urgent items. Ask your spouse to do the same. After your lists are complete, set aside a time in a neutral place, such as your favorite coffee shop, to go over your lists. See if together you can find a solution so that the starred items can be eliminated, made easier, or handled in a better way.

Otherwise, your relationship will suffer because you'll start withdrawing from each other. Remember: 60 percent of second marriages end in divorce because conflicts and resentments aren't resolved. The time you spend resolving the conflicts and setting your boundaries will help keep your relationship thriving.

# SAY SOMETHING POSITIVE
# ABOUT THE OTHER PARENT

One of the biggest hazards to a harmonious stepfamily is ongoing conflict with an ex-spouse. For children to make a positive adjustment following divorce and remarriage, they need a loving relationship with both parents. That means you must never criticize, put down, badmouth, or gossip about the other parent. You must not stand in the way of the biological parents' relationship with their children or with each other.

To begin with, don't call the other parent "the ex." That puts the focus on the failed marriage rather than the fact that the person is still the child's parent. Always call the person by his or her name.

Some people are very good about not badmouthing the other parent in front of the children, but still there's tension in the air. Without you ever muttering a nasty word, the children can sense the strain and animosity between you and the other parent. Living with bad vibes between Dad and Stepdad or between Mom and Stepmom is harmful to emotional and physical health. To avoid tension in the air, you may need to take the "No badmouthing policy" one step further: Give a sincere compliment to the children about their parent, for example, "You have pretty eyes, just like your Mother." When their mother comes to pick up the kids, invite her in and say something like, "You have wonderful children, you've done a great job as a parent," and as they leave be sure to say, "I hope you all have a wonderful time together."

Don't get caught in the crossfire of post-divorce animosity by fanning the flames of mistrust. You'll have to learn how to be cordial, and if you're fighting, you'll have to learn how to stop and start cooperating. Try to understand what life is like from the other parent's perspective. Instead of assuming John is being "Disneyland Dad" while you get all the dirty work, understand the fact that his apartment is so small, it's more enjoyable to take the kids on outings. When you don't understand, ask for clarification instead of jumping to conclusions. Honor your agreements, focus on solutions that work for the kids, and respect each household's autonomy.

The greatest gift you can give to your spouse and stepchildren is showing them that even after a family splits up, you can all emerge as a supportive expanded family unit. You pave the way for this healing by treating the other parent with consideration and kindness and by saying something positive.

# ASK (NICELY) FOR APPRECIATION

Stepparenting may be a thankless task in terms of verbal appreciation from your stepkids, but that doesn't mean you don't deserve appreciation. The truth is your that loving care of your mate's children—whether it is on the daily level or only during vacations—is an incredible gift of love for which he or she should be grateful.

Unfortunately, many parents feel so guilty about the burden that their children place on their new mates that they don't want even to think about the gift you are giving, much less thank you for it. This can be especially true if you, the stepparent, do not have children yourself. After all, if both of you are asking similar things of one another, the guilt is lessened—you're both having to deal with a child ignoring you or throwing things at you. But if you are the only one making the loving sacrifice, then the burden of guilt can be heavy indeed on your spouse. Chances are he is not an ingrate, but so much in your debt that he wants to avoid the subject altogether. That's just human nature. If you owed someone $10,000 and couldn't pay it back right now, would you want to run into them every day? Probably you'd go out of your way to avoid them.

As a consequence, rather than wallow in resentment, you may have to ask specifically (and nicely!) for appreciation for all you do for his or her children. "This was a big deal with Harvey and me," said Lisa, "and we had many fights in which he would try to deny that I deserved appreciation. He would argue that it was good for me and therefore I shouldn't need thanks. Finally, one day we went to therapy and the therapist looked him in the eye and said, 'Being a full-time mother of someone else's kid is a big deal and you should just get it. Right now.' That did it. From that point on, Harvey went out of his way to say thanks and every Mother's Day he writes me a note saying how grateful he is for all the love I show to his son."

You do deserve a big pat on the back for your job as a stepparent. Besides giving yourself a hand on a regular basis, it's okay to ask your partner for some appreciation. If a note of thanks would ring your chimes, let him know. If you'd love a backrub to acknowledge all you've done this week for her son, let her know. When it comes to appreciation, it never hurts to ask.

# BE WILLING TO BE FLEXIBLE

Parenting children requires a great deal of give and take: "Can you chauffeur Tina to the soccer game so I can take Lucy to her swim meet?" "Julia is sick; which of us can stay home more easily?" With stepkids, there are even more logistical issues to be worked out, particularly if there is joint custody. The whos, whats, and wheres expand exponentially when there are two (or more!) households to consider, and "yours, mine, and our" kids to consider. The whole delicate balance can be thrown into a tailspin, unless you are all willing to be flexible.

Nowhere is this more true than in the emotionally charged issue of holiday planning. You've agreed to alternate having the kids on Christmas Day, and this year it's your turn—but her family is having the first reunion of all their relatives in twenty years and so she wants them this year again. Or it's her turn, and you've planned a romantic trip to Hawaii just for the two of you, and suddenly she's in the hospital and you have to cancel your plans and take the kids. Or he just doesn't show up to take the kids on Father's Day as promised.

These all can be hot-button issues, potential flashpoints between you and your spouse, between your spouse and the ex, between you and the kids, or any permutation thereof. It's easy when plans go awry, especially holiday plans, for the people involved to lose their tempers and get very rigid: "He always leaves us in the lurch." "We're always the ones doing the chauffeuring." "No way am I going to ruin my vacation to accommodate her!" While such feelings are natural and may even be appropriate, they don't do a lot for resolving the situation in a manner that maximizes the potential for happiness.

Flexibility—and an eye on what's most important—will help defuse most of these potential trouble spots. Why can't you celebrate Christmas on December 26? By doing it joyfully, you'll have a better time, and the kids won't have to live in a morass of hostility and anger.

"Fred's ex-wife refused to do her share of shuttling the kids back and forth," remembers Rosemary. "She claimed that since the divorce was his idea, we would have to do all of the driving, about ninety miles round-trip each Friday evening to pick up his daughter and each Sunday evening to bring her back. Of course it was grossly unfair. But Fred always said that seeing his daughter was more important than being right, and because I love him, I help out as much as I can." Flexibility is the ability to roll with the punches—and since stepparenting is full of punches, we should all limber up!

# ENCOURAGE A HEALTHY RELATIONSHIP WITH THE EX-SPOUSE

Maybe you and your mate get along just fine with your exes. If so, congratulations! That makes life much easier, not only for you but for your kids. But unfortunately, many of us harbor great anger or resentment toward the person we used to be married to, or the person who used to be married to our current spouse, and that can make life quite unpleasant, especially for the young ones.

When you choose to have children with someone, you are not only making a lifelong commitment to your children, but you also are creating a lifelong tie to their other parent, whether you choose to acknowledge it or not. When we hang on to anger and refuse to forgive our former spouse, or encourage our current spouse to be angry and bitter, we prevent the full creation of the loving family we desire now. As the Sufis say, "As long as there is room in your heart for one enemy, your heart isn't a safe place for a friend."

We can't control what our ex or our spouse's ex will do. But we can practice from a distance being openhearted toward them and blessing them on their journey. And because we may have less volatile feelings toward our mate's ex, we can also encourage him or her to forgive if necessary.

Such encouragement can reap beautiful rewards. We know a woman in her twenties, Louise, who was very resentful toward her stepmother of four years. She didn't like her and didn't intend to try. Then Louise got engaged and began to plan her wedding. One day her father, holding onto his anger over his divorce from Louise's mother more than ten years before, proclaimed that he would not contribute a cent to the wedding if Louise's mother were present. Louise was in despair, threatening to elope and angry that her parents couldn't come together in peace even for her wedding day. About a week later, she got a call from her father. He had changed his mind. "I know that my stepmother worked on him," Louise told us. Suddenly she saw her stepmother in a whole new light and their relationship has finally taken off.

Practice and encourage forgiveness—if only for the sake of the kids.

# NEGOTIATE RELATIONSHIPS
# WITH RELATIVES

One of the fall-outs from divorce is not just changed relationships between parents and kids, but between kids and their grandparents and other relatives. Depending on the situation, grandparents can suddenly find themselves out in the cold, unable to see or talk to their beloved grandchildren. This can send them into a panic and set them against you, the interloper whom they believe is standing in their way.

As a stepparent, you can do both your kids and their extended family a big favor by encouraging continuing relationships with the ex's relatives. "One of the consequences of being a stepmother that I never would have foreseen," says Nancy, "is a very strong relationship with Fred's ex–mother-in-law. She knows I am a good caretaker of her grandchildren and that I encourage her relationship with the kids, and she appreciates that. As a consequence, she would do almost anything for me."

Every kid needs as many people to love him, to nurture her, as possible, and we stepparents must not only acknowledge the truth of that, but we must also work with our spouses to make sure the extended family's bonds remain strong. This might mean anything from letting the kids go to Grandma Pat's on Easter rather than be with you, to creating occasions at your house where the steprelatives can come and see the kids.

Only you and your spouse know what is best for you and your kids. But don't let bad feelings stand in your way of encouraging as much connection as possible. Don't assume that the grandparents know that they are welcome. Tell them in a letter or in person that you want them to stay involved in the grandkids' lives. If they live out of town, follow through by sending pictures.

Kinship is a connection by blood, marriage, or adoption; it's a relationship among people who have an affinity for one another. Perhaps your stepson, Josh, is close friends with his cousin who is the nephew of your husband's former wife. The friendship between Josh and his cousin doesn't go away just because his parents are no longer married. Kinship is the branching out of the nuclear family. When you took on a stepfamily, whether you noticed it right off the bat or it took you a while to feel the impact, the fact is you've not only got next-of-kin, you've got widespread, far-reaching kinships.

Take pride in all your connections. Honor the depth and breadth of the entire family unit. You'll develop many surprising resources to call in a crisis, if you do.

# KEEP THE KIDS OUT
# OF THE MIDDLE

Most likely, the children under your care are in a difficult situation vis-à-vis their two sets of parents. They know, if only intuitively, if there is any tension between them, and often feel it is their responsibility to smooth the waters and create peace. But because the problem is an adult one and not of their making, they can never truly restore harmony, and therefore the children can end up feeling like failures.

Kids have a tendency to feel responsible for whatever goes wrong between the adults in their lives, but we can make their lives as painless as possible if we agree with our spouse to keep the kids out of the middle—out of the middle of any disagreement between the two of us, and out of the middle of any muddles between us and their other parent.

Patricia can't stand her ex-husband, so instead of dealing with him directly, she uses her fourteen-year-old daughter, Paige, as the go-between. Paige hates the position because her dad uses guilt and bribery to manipulate her into doing what he wants. Patricia is afraid of his temper, so has defaulted on her responsibility to protect her daughter from such conflicts. But as the adults, you must shield the children from the warfare.

This means, of course, remembering that "little pitchers have big ears" and to confine our grousing about the exes till the kids are truly out of earshot. And it means not using the child as a conduit between the two of us in a fight—"Tell your mother I am furious she bought the new dishwasher without consulting me," or "Tell your stepfather he is a stingy pig"—and, most important, not using the child as a messenger between our house and the ex's. No telling the kids to ask Dad for the support check or to ask Mom to change the pick-up arrangements for next week. If you need to change the arrangements, call her directly. If you're concerned about all the clothes you bought for little Emily that she took back to Dad's and you haven't seen since, call him and ask that the clothes be sent back next time.

We shouldn't ask the children to do our dirty work for us; after all, we are the adults here and so should shoulder the burden. Make a pact with your spouse to keep the kids out of the middle. The children will be better off for it.

# TALK ABOUT
# FINANCIAL CONCERNS

Money is a hot spot for any couple, and the realities of stepfamilies only make it more so. Child-support payments you or your spouse must make, ex-spouses' failures to pay child support, the myriad of items you, the stepparent, end up providing for your stepchildren—any or all of these can cause resentment or open warfare.

We once knew a couple, Grace and Charles, who broke up over his resentment concerning money. Grace had three kids from a former marriage and an ex who failed to make his child-support payments. In the beginning, Charles, who was childless, was willing to take up the slack. But over the years it got to him. "While Grace did work, her job did not cover the expenses of three kids. I was keeping the family together financially and not getting any credit for it, from either Grace or the kids. I was resentful and began having affairs as a way to exert my independence. I got tired of it being so lopsided financially—I even bought a house that we could all live in—and so when I met Louise, who had no children, I just took off. I'm sorry that I never was able to tell Grace how I felt, but every time I tried, she brushed me off."

Money issues are never easy to talk about, particularly if the truth is that you feel resentful about the situation with your spouse. It's hard to own up to such feelings—they may seem petty or selfish. But as Charles' story demonstrates, if you let the situation fester, it can cause an irreparable breach in your relationship. So first, ask yourself some hard questions: Is the financial situation you find yourself in fair? If not, who is carrying more of the burden? How do you and he or she truly feel about that? Does the situation call for some creative thinking?

We know a couple, a childless woman and a man with a son, who resolved the problem uniquely. "We each contribute the exact same amount to our household expenses," says Mary Ellen, "and keep the rest for ourselves. Then I don't worry about what Bob is spending on his son. He does what he wants with the rest of his money and so do I."

Finding creative solutions depends first on acknowledging that there might be inequities that are causing bad feelings. So be honest with yourself first and then with your spouse—don't let money come between you.

# SEEK HELP WHEN NECESSARY

As much as the two of you love one another, communicate about the difficult things, and try to remain flexible and lighthearted, you may encounter situations that require outside help. Please don't feel badly about needing help—as we have said before, this is hard. And sometimes an outside perspective or suggestion is just what makes the difference.

"We could not have survived the first couple years," recalls Anna, "without our therapist. Bill and I were completely oblivious to the issues that divorce and remarriage with kids would raise. Plus we still had issues within our relationship to work out. Week after week we discovered that we weren't alone in confronting these problems and learned the negotiating skills we needed to communicate well with one another."

The following symptoms are indications you could benefit from professional assistance: 1) You and your partner are frequently locked into bitter conflict and arguments. 2) You feel depressed and hopeless about your situation. 3) Family conflicts lead to physical threats or violence. 4) One child in your family has been identified as the "troublemaker." 5) One or both of you is using drugs or alcohol to cope. 6) A child is having problems in school or with peers. 7) You get little or no satisfaction from family life.

Don't get bound up in denial. Emotional distress is prolonged if you ignore it. Whether you choose individual therapy, couples or family counseling, pastoral advice, or a support group depends on your situation and temperament.

Sandra and Greg, married four years, came to counseling with Judy because stepson Jeff was flunking out of junior high. They argued incessantly about how to deal with him—Greg wanted to send Jeff to live with his biological father; Sandra felt Greg was shirking his commitment to her by wanting her son out of the picture. Initially they thought if counseling could "fix Jeff" their family life would improve. After an initial evaluation they designed a treatment approach that included a stepparenting support group, brief marriage counseling, extra tutoring for Jeff, and single nights out for each of them. They put in considerable effort to face their problems. In the support group, they learned conflict resolution skills and made friends with others in the same boat. In marriage counseling they learned more productive ways of communicating. Tutoring gave Jeff a boost to his self-esteem because his grades went up and took the parents out of the homework battles. Single nights out relieved the tension of never having time for reflecting or relaxing with friends.

Seeking outside help is not a sign of weakness but rather a sign of your loving intention to do all that you can to heal the wounds, right the wrongs, and be responsible parents and loving partners.

# MAKE TIME FOR
# THE TWO OF YOU

This is one of the unique challenges blended families present to us. When we fall in love and are childless, there is usually a period of time in which we get to be alone with our beloved, basking in our newfound love and learning about all of his or her idiosyncrasies. Moonlit walks, long dinners, uninterrupted hours for lovemaking ... all of the delicious togetherness that is the mortar that holds the bricks of our relationship together.

But with children on the scene, such togetherness—if it can be accomplished at all in the courtship phase with baby-sitters and the ex-spouse's visitation schedule—is usually short-lived.Soon there you are—all together and often none too happy about it. "That is one of the real challenges of our relationship," says Shirley, whose husband has three kids who live with them full-time. "Because Mick is a widower, we didn't have more than two minutes alone before I met the kids. I like them and we get along pretty well, but I still long for time for just the two of us. I mean, sometimes it seems as though the three of them are purposely trying never to give us a minute alone."

Unless you are a very occasional stepparent, you probably have feelings similar to Shirley's. Every couple needs time alone, but somehow when it is the other person's children who are standing in the way, it's easy to feel particularly resentful.

There are all kinds of ways to find the time, no matter what your financial circumstances. "Bill and I go out to dinner alone once a week," says Anna. "That's our special time." Stephanie and Don drop their kids off at Grandma's for the weekend four times a year and take off in their trailer. Stuart and Liz use the time when the kids are at their other parents' house to reconnect again.

It doesn't matter how you do it; what matters is that you take the time to do it. Remember—it was your love for this person that got you into the situation in the first place. Nurture that love and the rest will be easier.

# OFFER PRIVATE TIME TO KIDS AND THEIR PARENTS

When the Sanchez family came to counseling, they were eager to find better ways to live harmoniously together. It took only a few sessions to identify one of the fallacies they had been operating under. The parents thought that in order to make a successful adjustment as a blended household, they should no longer spend time alone with their biological kids. They worried that if they spent one-on-one time with their own kids, the others would be jealous and that would drive a wedge between them.

While talking this over, the Sanchezes discovered that this mistaken notion was actually creating more friction in their household. Maria missed the private outings and the mother-daughter talks that she and Anna had shared for the previous six years when they lived alone. José longed for boys' nights and camping weekends with his twins. With the best of intentions Maria and José had stopped all separate outings for fear the others might feel left out. They admitted to missing their private time with their own kids. It turns out that the kids also longed for alone time with their biological parents. When the Sanchezes reinstated the outings and allowed for private moments, they all felt the sadness disappearing. By hanging out as they had done before they were a blended family, everyone felt less of a sense of loss and more energy when they were all together.

Becoming a stepfamily is a wonderful event, but it's also accompanied by loss. The loss of privacy, the loss of a previous way of life, the loss of routine, and the loss of the familiar. Perhaps it also means loss of friends because of a move to a new neighborhood or new city. You'll lessen the loss when you allow for private time between parent and child. Just as you need time alone with your spouse to keep your relationship thriving, the kids need time to fortify the love and communication with their parent.

Be sensitive to the need for private talks and one-on-one outings. No matter how much you like the stepchildren, or they like you, they still need time alone with your spouse. "Sometimes just a smidgen of privacy with their mom makes a big difference in the way the kids are treating me," says Hank. "I don't mind when my stepdaughter Brynn goes out to dinner alone with her dad," says Rene. "It's a treat for both of them and, besides it gives me some much-needed solitude."

Try not to feel threatened by your stepchild's need for personal moments with his or her parent. Offer to give them privacy by saying, "I can see you'd like to talk in private." Make yourself scarce. Tell them it's okay with you so that they don't feel guilty. Your stepkids and partner will appreciate your mature generosity, and you can have a quiet house all to yourself.

# WALK A MILE IN YOUR
# SPOUSE'S SHOES

Empathy is the capacity to feel the reality of another person's situation, even though it is different from yours. It is an expansion of the heart, an act of love that says even though I'm over here in my circumstance, I am aware of and concerned for you over there in your circumstance.

For us stepparents, empathy helps us stay connected to our spouse through the various ups and downs that the children in our lives will create. It helps us remember that while it is hard for us that little Jillian won't speak to us, it is also hard for her father, our beloved. How must it feel when your own flesh and blood tells your wife, whom you love deeply, that she hates her? How must it feel when the son you care for so much refuses to sit down at the same table with your husband? We of course feel badly if these things happen, but our spouse, whose child is acting so badly, must feel terrible too. "It hurts deeply to see my son and husband fighting. I can't even explain the agony of seeing the two most precious people in my life calling each other names and refusing to cooperate," Helena told her stepparenting group.

If you're having difficulty empathizing with your spouse's position, try this simple exercise. Take a five-minute break, sit in a quiet corner, close your eyes, and bring your partner into focus. Think about their day and all that they are doing. Look at their face and imagine what life is like from their perspective. What is it like to entrust the care of your child to another person? What is it like when their child is unhappy? In group, Wayne, along with other stepparents, came to a new awareness of Helena's pain when he did this exercise. As the stepparents began to view home life from their spouses' perspective, they understood that the biological parent often feels on the verge of another disastrous failure when there are hurtful encounters between their beloved spouse and precious child. They feel sad, helpless, and deeply troubled.

When we remember his or her pain, rather than just focusing on our own, we allow our hearts to open in love toward our spouse. Rather than seeing them as the enemy who got us into the horrid situation in the first place, we are able to see them as fellow travelers on this particular journey. Like us, he is trying the best he knows how; she is doing the best she can. When we walk a mile in our beloved's shoes we can be truly grateful for the priceless treasure of the child we are sharing.

# LOOK FOR THE BLESSINGS

To thrive as a stepparent requires courage, character, and commitment for sure, but it also calls you to count your blessings, see the positive, and look for the silver linings. The positive side of human nature is a mighty force, and when you cultivate its potential you can turn the gloomiest situation bright. The folks who succeed in the stepparenting department do so in large part because of their ability to see the positive and to be grateful for the tiniest of blessings.

Maintaining a positive, upbeat attitude is a core ingredient in winning in any situation. If you believe that your living situation is "awful" you will probably create unhappy interactions. Likewise if you channel your inner thoughts and spoken words to encouraging ideas and uplifting suggestions, your life will take on a positive aura. When you get up in the morning and believe that today is going to be a great day with your stepkids and spouse, and that tomorrow will be even greater, you see to it that it happens.

Think back to when you met and dated your spouse. What drew you to him or her in the first place? When you met the children, what were the warm feelings you had? Now write down five blessings that these souls have brought into your life. Describe the joy and excitement that's been added to your life because of them.

Be specific about the blessings you're receiving. Say them out loud at the dinner table, whisper them in your sweetheart's ear, leave a note pasted to the bathroom mirror for everyone to read. List the blessings in your journal each night for one month. If you know you have to write them down, you'll get into the habit of looking for the joy.

Keep your eyes open for the tiniest windfalls. "On Father's Day we gave Will a list of the many blessings we received from having him in our life," recall Judy and Amanda. "We wrote down that he taught us to appreciate the Beatles and Mozart, how to cook veggie burgers, and the advantages of eating with chopsticks." Be sure to tell your sweetheart often how much they've enriched your lives.

"As soon as Matt and I got home, we began recounting the horrors and imagined mistreatment of our day, until that was all we were seeing," said Christine. "Then while watching *Oprah*, I learned about keeping a grateful journal, which changed the way I view my blended family. Each day I list three things I'm grateful for—watching Jake read a bedtime story to my daughter, seeing the love on his face when his son calls, listening as he teaches our son to play the guitar."

By dwelling on the unhappy incidents of yesterday, you end up wallowing in pain and apprehension missing the pleasure of the moment. In this moment, right now, can you see the beauty and the blessings surrounding you and your spouse?

# INTERACTING WITH THE KIDS

*We learn to do something by doing it.*
*There is no other way.*

—John Holt

# ASSUME THE BEST

Even though four-year-old Amanda didn't see her father regularly, she wasn't about to accept Will as a stand-in. In fact, the first time she met him she opened the front door, kicked him as hard as she could, and loudly warned, "Leave my mother alone." Fortunately, he was good-natured and understanding about it; he rather admired her spunk. "Even though I was mortified," remembers Judy, "he remained positive, appreciating her directness and spirit. In the ensuing years, no matter how she ignored him, scowled at him, or frowned, he always assumed the best about her. Eventually she saw him as her ally."

Children of divorce suffer setbacks to self-esteem and their sense of security is shaken. Often plagued by guilt and shame, they feel responsible for their parents' divorce. They've lost a portion of childhood innocence and are forced to deal with adult issues before they have appropriate skills for the task. They worry that something else might go wrong, and they may feel pessimistic. These anxieties and worries are frequently acted out in troublesome behaviors. If you recognize the depth of the despair children can feel when biological parents no longer live together, you won't misinterpret your stepchild's sullenness, orneryness, or belligerence as character flaws, and you won't take it personally.

Bad behavior is frequently evidence of fear, confusion, frustration, and insecurity. If you view your stepson as a "little creep" who is trying to make your life miserable, you'll set a pessimistic tone for your entire relationship. When you assume the worse, you put a negative spin on a perfectly normal emotional process, unpleasant behavior is magnified, and your relationship becomes bogged down in misunderstanding.

You can assist your stepchild in resolving his upset by assuming the best. "It's confusing to have a stepfather" is better than "Don't ignore me when I talk to you." If you point out his cranky disposition, he'll get stuck believing that's all there is about him, and things will rapidly slide downhill. The worse your stepchild is behaving, the more he needs your kindness, recognition, and genuine appreciation. By assuming the best, the best can blossom.

Believe that your problem is solvable, expect good things to come, and don't put energy into figuring out who is right or who is wrong. How you view the child will make a difference, because when you assume the best you create an environment in which children feel safe and respected. In such an environment defensive behaviors melt, and your stepchildren are able to open their hearts and let you in.

# ALLOW THEM TO EXPRESS
# HOW THEY FEEL

Feelings are incredibly powerful. In his book *Emotional Intelligence*, Daniel Goleman describes research that shows that most of our reactions to things—our likes and dislikes, our fears and angers—are controlled by the most primitive part of our brains, which operate in an instinctive way to protect us. The most advanced part of the brain, the neocortex, is engaged only if we pause between feeling and reaction to think about the various consequences of acting on our feelings. Unless we do pause, we are responding instinctively, based on patterns that were laid down in the earliest years of childhood. That's why one of the components of emotional intelligence, says Goleman, is an ability to identify our feelings and have some choice in how and when we express them.

As caretakers of children, it is one of our sacred duties to develop emotional intelligence in ourselves and pass those skills along. Nowhere is this more valuable than in helping our children deal with the strong feelings being part of a blended family can create. First, we can teach children to recognize their feelings—"I'm mad; I'm sad; I'm glad"—and then begin to see that feelings are just energy in motion that we can choose to do something about or not.

One process that might help your family situation is the use of a talking stick. This is an American Indian tradition in which people sit in a circle. When a person feels moved to speak, she holds the "talking stick." While she is holding the stick, she has the floor and no one can interrupt or rebut what she is saying. The rest of the circle must listen in silence. When she is done, someone else can take up the stick, but he too must speak from the heart. Again no one can rebut, deny, disagree with, or counter anyone else's truth. Rather it is up to the listeners to simply receive what the speaker is saying.

This is a great way for kids to get their feelings out about a situation they find themselves in and for them to begin to understand that their feelings are just that—feelings. If you do it often enough, they will begin to see that their feelings change—hate one day might be mild dislike another; love might be there one day and not the next. As they begin to see their feelings as a river on which they can witness themselves, a flow on which their consciousness rests but is somehow separate from, they can begin to ride the currents of feelings more graciously. And as they see that you are able to receive their feelings, no matter how "horrible," without being destroyed, they will begin to use their feelings less as weapons and more as vehicles for connection.

# DO A PHYSICAL
# ACTIVITY TOGETHER

As a stepparent you'll often feel as if you're in the middle of a nightmare in which you're the last person chosen to play on the team. The trick for feeling better is to find ways to have fun together even when you're not sure anyone wants you there in the first place. Physical activity—games, horsing around, and goofing off—are the quickest, most productive ways to bond as a expanded family.

Perhaps you've gotten so caught up in the day-to-day grind of keeping your blended household operating that you've forgotten about having a good time. Often stepparents want so much to be accepted that they're hypersensitive to rejection. In fact they become oversensitive, seeing rejection in every action. If you recognize this tendency in yourself, the best way to overcome it to discover each other through free, noncompetitive, lighthearted, robust play. Add a daily dose of silliness, dancing, singing, and smiling to your routine. By placing your emphasis on having fun rather than making your life together ideal, you can avoid many wicked stepparent pitfalls.

Everyone wins when you're having fun. Doing physical activities once a week is a good way to ignite the joy that holds a family together. A hardy workout lets off steam and melts anger in nonhurtful ways. You can soothe rivalries and resentments through a game of tennis, baseball, tag, or by playing hide-and-seek. Climb trees, walk in the rain and splash in puddles, go for a hike, take square dancing lessons, go bicycling, try rollerblading. Get out of the house and jump around. It's vital to your emerging family to communicate about the nitty-gritty and nuances of combining your lives, but remember that communication is frequently best when it's unspoken. You don't have to talk endlessly about all the problems; sometimes it's better to keep your frustrations to yourself and work it out by playing hard.

Try dividing up the teams so that each child gets to be on a team once with their own parent and once with the stepparent. Try having siblings together first, and then try mix-matched sets. You burn off excess energy and resolve unspoken conflicts with a friendly water fight.

Put on the boogie-woogie music and prance around before dinner. Sing a song while peeling the potatoes, turn off the television, and get the music blaring. Soon everyone will be tapping their toes, and you'll all forget at least for a moment that you're not blood-related. It's impossible to be sour when you're playing volleyball, laughing, whistling, and horsing around.

# ACKNOWLEDGE THE TRUTH
# OF THEIR SITUATION

The truth is incredibly powerful, and we should never underestimate its value in dealing with kids. So often adults have a tendency to sugarcoat things when talking to kids, to "put the best face on it," to evade or even downright lie. But kids are truth-seeking missiles—the more we tell the truth, and even more important, acknowledge the truth of their situation, the more they will respect us and treat us well in return.

This means saying, "Yes, I understand that you don't want to be here. It must be hard to have to shuffle between houses just because a judge said so" when a child complains about the arrangements, rather than, "Now come on, it will be fun," or, "You don't mean that," or even worse, "That makes me feel bad." (It's your job as the adult to take care of them, not to ask them to take care of you and your feelings.) Let's face it—they are in a tough situation. Would you like to have to live in two places and move back and forth on alternate weeks? Or up and go to another house every fourth weekend?

Kids need their feelings validated, not ignored, denied, or overrun by your feelings, and children in stepfamilies have some pretty tough feelings to deal with. The truth is they didn't ask to be in your life any more than you asked them to be in yours, and the fact that they are can create strong feelings of anger, jealousy, or even guilt. As step-parents, we need to validate the truth of how they feel.

"My proudest moment as a stepparent," remembers Anna, "came when Zoe was about twelve. Her brother was living with us full-time by then, but she was still with her mother and visiting us every other weekend. We were having a pleasant dinner and I had just made some innocuous comment. She turned and said, 'Why don't you go away and never come back.' I was terribly hurt and shocked. She and I had always had a wonderful, close relationship for over ten years. This seemed to come out of the blue. I remained quiet and let a couple of hours pass so I could think about the situation. Suddenly it came to me. She was jealous of the fact that her brother was living with us full-time and guilty over not wanting to be with her mother. If I disappeared, she wouldn't be having such feelings. I went up to her room, took her into my arms and very quietly said, 'I think sometimes you wish you were my little girl and could live here all the time.' She burst into tears, and we hugged for a long time. Nothing else was said, but we never had another difficult moment."

Sometimes acknowledging the truth of the situation is very simple: "Yes I see you are very angry." Other times, as Anna's story demonstrates, it requires going below the surface to touch the deeper truth. Either way, our commitment to the truth will help guide us moment to moment.

# BE PREPARED FOR
# THE COLD SHOULDER

If you are new at this, you might be surprised if you get a less than totally enthusiastic response from your stepkids. After all, they're great, as their parent, your spouse, has told you, and you know you're great, so what's the problem? The problem, of course, is that they may have very complex feelings that you have no awareness of about the situation: Stacey has enjoyed being the "woman" in Daddy's life for several years and now you've come along to replace her; Tim has feelings of hostility toward all women because of his relationship with his mother, and you are now a convenient target; you are being blamed for the divorce by your wife's ex who is teaching the kids actively to hate you. Any number of things could be—and are—going on.

At the very least, the kids are wary—Is this man going to try to replace my father? Is she going to treat me fairly or will she show favoritism to her own kids? Will I get time with my father or will he be so absorbed by her that he will ignore me? None of this is a recipe for instant intimacy, and you shouldn't expect it. Until they've figured out where they stand, and have gotten to know and trust you at least a bit, be prepared for the cold shoulder. This could range anywhere from a certain cool, polite formality—"Yes, Mrs. Cleaver, I do like math," to favoritism—Kim holds Daddy's hand crossing the street, but won't take yours—all the way to downright hostility: "I hate you and wish you'd drop dead."

So many of us enter stepparenting expecting the best—and that's good, a positive attitude is important—that we get thrown completely by the cold shoulder, fearing that it will go on forever. Chances are it won't—especially if you don't take it too seriously and continue to be your kind, funny, down-to-earth self. If we get on our high horse— I'm your stepmother now and you *must* love me—or if we try and force intimacy before they are ready—It's *so* wonderful that we can be together, kiss, kiss—the cold shoulder will escalate or harden into a perpetual stance.

In a way, being a stepparent is a little like wooing someone who's reluctant to get into a relationship. Too much intimacy or too many demands and they will get scared off. Just the right touch of friendliness and care, a bit of mystery and humor, and they will come running to your side. Well, eventually, anyway.

# GIVE THEM TIME

This is a corollary to "Be prepared for the Cold Shoulder." Everyone needs time to develop positive feelings toward other people, and just because you have become (or are about to become) these children's stepparent doesn't mean they will love you right away. They need time to adjust to the reality of the new situation and to understand their place in it. With time they will see that you are fair and on their side. With time, they will see that you are great at games, or a good listener, or just the person to help them with their writing assignments. In other words, with time, they will see you more and more for who you really are, rather than merely a blank screen for their fear and anger.

This doesn't mean you will necessarily have the kind of close relationship that you might truly want, but that you will both be able to accept one another and live in basic harmony. "Michael was cold to me for the first couple years of my being in his life," says Anna. "But as time went on, he grew to accept, and, I think, even love me in his own way. I was the one to turn to for homework help, the one who was always there if he needed something. We were never as close as Zoe and I have been, but we were able to live peaceably with one another. Several times he made me birthday or Mother's Day cards in which he expressed strong feelings that he was uncomfortable verbalizing. I used to feel bad about it, but after talking to lots of parents of boys, ultimately, I don't think it is any different than many mother-son relationships."

As Anna's story demonstrates, relating to our stepchildren is a lot like relating to our relatives. Some we may feel incredibly close to; toward others we feel a warmth; still others are a challenge to connect with. Somehow, with time, we learn to accept them all, relishing the deep closeness we feel toward some and appreciating the good parts of those who are a challenge to us.

By giving our stepchildren time to grow to like and love us, by not panicking if the warm feelings don't flow immediately, we give them the psychological space they need to make us part of their family. Maybe we'll end up as a cherished parent, or perhaps be thought of more like an eccentric, but beloved aunt. But as we continue in their lives, we will end up being accepted as "part of the family."

# TEACH RESPECT

While you're acknowledging the truth of the situation, expecting the cold shoulder, and giving them time, this doesn't mean that you have to put up with maltreatment. Your stepkids don't have to love you or even like you, but you do have the right to ask for the kind of respect any other human being would receive. You may have to teach them how to give it to you.

Teaching respect begins with an internalized attitude—it says, "I know that I will not allow myself to be walked all over as doormat, but neither am I so afraid that I *am* a doormat that I see disrespect in every little action." Rather it is a quiet self-assuredness that requests that you be treated well.

This can be tricky territory, because it's easy in the heat of the moment to feel disrespect from a hostile stepchild and to find yourself in a pitched battle over being treated well. The trick is not to let it become an adversarial situation, but through your (and your spouse's) modeling of respect for one another and the children, you set the example for how you want to be treated.

Sometimes this doesn't work, and you find yourself in a direct confrontation. You and Tommy are alone and you have just asked him to pick up his toys and he has replied, "You're not my mother, I don't have to listen to you." Probably, you and your spouse have come to an agreement already about this—for example, Tommy must pick up his toys before dinner when he is in our house—as well as agreed upon a strategy for noncompliance—no dessert, say. So what do you do?

What *not* to do is to start yelling back about how you deserve respect as his stepmother. Instead, if you acknowledge the truth of the situation and in your firm, yet calm control, things should go pretty well: "You're right, I'm not your mother, and I can't make you pick up your toys, but right now you are here. One of our house rules, as you know, is that you pick up your toys before dinner. If you don't you won't get dessert. It's your choice."

Teaching respect can range from refusing to answer unless addressed in a civil manner (which you announce in a very neutral voice) to saying something like "Ouch" when a stepchild makes a hurtful comment. Exactly what to do when is something you need to feel your way through. You don't have to stand for abuse—but don't make a federal case over it. Again, lightheartedness is your ally.

# RESPECT THEIR LIKES AND DISLIKES

To earn respect from our stepchildren, we must show it to them in return. This can be difficult when they are being mean to you. One simple way to establish a sense of respect is to discover their likes and dislikes and then try to honor them when the stepchildren are with you.

Jason doesn't like eggs? Rather than ridiculing that or trying to get him to broaden his culinary horizons, offer pancakes with a remark such as, "I know you don't like eggs, so I've made pancakes just for you." Jennifer hates pink, your favorite color. Offer to go to the hardware store with her to find a color for her room that she will enjoy.

It should go without saying that we try to please those we live with by indulging their little idiosyncracies, but somehow, as a stepparent, the likes and dislikes of our stepchildren can be annoying. Perhaps it is because we don't have a long history with these children yet; we weren't there when little Mark caught his first fish on a trip with Dad and now is a fishing fanatic. It just seems like a boring waste of time to us. We weren't present when baby Megan first took her stuffed bunny to bed at six months; all we know now, eight years later, is that the thing is torn and smells and "she's too old" for such a thing.

When we respect our stepkids' likes and dislikes, when we go out of our way to plan the fishing trip, serve food without onions, or let him sleep with the fan on in the winter because the noise is soothing, we demonstrate our care. We show them that we see who they are and that who they are matters to us. We also show that this arrangement is not just a one-way street. They may have to come to our house and live by our *policies*, but we are willing to change and adapt for them too. We're willing to give up chicken on the bone, the chance to sleep late on weekends, an orderly guest room, because the stepkids are important to us.

Parents make such accommodations all the time and kids don't generally even consciously notice. We stepparents are coming in later in the game and have to play catch-up. It's okay to point the adaptations you've made out—as long as you do it in a loving, non-guilt trip way. These gestures go a long way toward demonstrating our concern for their happiness and well-being. What little thing can you do to make your stepchild feel loved today?

# DO IT THEIR WAY WHEN YOU CAN

Children cooperate more easily and behave more responsibly when given a choice in the matters that affect them, such as visitation, phone calls, and scheduled activities. Involving children in age-appropriate decision-making gives them a feeling of security, a sense of belonging, and helps them feel less a helpless casualty of divorce and more in control of their lives.

Residential custody with one parent is best for children under the age of five. They need the routine that a primary caretaker provides. As children grow, they can adjust to spending more time with the noncustodial parents, but they still need to be informed about when visits will occur, what activities are planned, and what the schedule might be. Older children deserve to have input into changes the parents are considering. School-age kids have friends, school activities, and social schedules that need to be taken into consideration. Teens may express a desire to move and live with another parent. Such wishes call for your thoughtful examination without making the child feel guilty or disloyal.

When fifteen-year-old Kristie, who lived with her mother and stepfather from age four, decided she wanted to go live with her father, her mother was shaken initially, but her stepfather recognized the courage it took for her to voice her desire. He understood that her need to live with her dad was sincere, and he empathized with her emotional struggle to keep everyone satisfied. He helped her sort through the pros and cons and negotiate a workable solution.

In the blending of households, and the juggling of visitation, kids often feel they have no rights. In some ways this is true, because the adults are making so many decisions on behalf of the child. To minimize their feelings of helplessness, give them as much control as you can over the little things.

For example, Will wanted to attend Amanda's fourth-grade concert, but Amanda wasn't thrilled about having him there. "If you'd rather go with just your mother, that's okay with me," he said. After thinking it over, she said he could come on one condition—"that you wear your suit." Will seldom wore a suit but for that occasion, he willingly obliged her.

His willingness to do it her way set the tone for the give-and-take required when families blend. When possible, he would do things the way she preferred—drive down her "favorite street" on the way to school, or let her choose the music in the car. He told her, "I do things for you because you do things for me. You turn your music down when it gets too loud and you get off the phone when I need to make a call." He was careful to acknowledge all she did for him. And likewise when possible, he would honor her requests and preferences.

# USE YOUR INTUITION

You've probably already figured out that despite all the books claiming to tell you what to do, all the childrearing theories, there are no rules in parenting—or in stepparenting. It all depends on the situation and the people involved. That's why some of our suggestions are followed by their opposites—often both are true, sometimes even at the same time!

Recognizing the truth of this can be nerve-wracking, because we want to do the right thing and wish there were hard and fast rules that we could just learn and follow. But the truth is that every soul is different, and what he or she needs may be different from what anyone else needs, and may also be different moment by moment, day by day. That's what makes parenting so fascinating—you can't just figure it out once and for all. One day she needs slack, the next day a tight rein. One time he needs you to hold the line; another time he needs you to look the other way. Debbie responds to your care and attention by blossoming like a flower; Tina withers you with a glance if you try the same approach on her.

So what's a (step)parent to do? Besides getting good advice, we believe that you can only ever do two things: really get to know who this person is; and then follow your intuition. The more you understand the children under your care—*really* understand, not create stories that get in the way of understanding—the more you can read the signals moment to moment as they come up and follow what your heart tells you to do: now I should ask the delicate question; now I should keep my mouth shut; now I should request some time alone; now I should be there for him.

Unless you are tuned in to your stepchildren, you will be traveling blind, destined to make many wrong turns. But once you do tune in, you will be amazed what your intuition will begin to show you: Tom is angry and he thinks he's mad at me. If I go give him a hug, he'll feel better and the whole problem will blow over; Samantha needs someone to talk to, she's worried about something she can't tell her parents. Here's where I can finally be of help.

Following your intuition means staying openhearted toward your stepkids, no matter how they are behaving, for the information won't flow well if you are closed off to them. If you can remember you are in their lives in service to their souls, you will always be able to find your way back to them, no matter what is going on. From there, your heart will tell you what to do.

# FIND A WAY TO CONNECT

"When I was feeling particularly estranged from Michael," remembers Anna, "a friend of mine asked me what he was really interested in. 'Physics,' I replied. 'He really wants to be the next Albert Einstein.' 'So,' she said, 'if I were you, I'd learn all I could about physics—or at least Einstein. That way you will be able to meet him in an area of *his* interest.'

"What great advice. It was true that we had virtually no mutual interests. He loved baseball; I hated it. He loved science fiction; I hated it. I loved hot tubs and swimming and he was uncomfortable in water. No wonder we weren't connected—we had nothing in common! Now physics was also something I had less than zero interest in, but I did want to improve our relationship and I was fascinated by the person of Albert Einstein. So I got a biography and began to talk to him about it."

All healthy relationships have what therapist Daphne Rose Kingma calls the medium of connection—something that brings you together and keeps you together in the rough spots of a relationship. It can be anything—fishing, shopping, talking about feelings, gardening, windsurfing, taking long walks, reading books and talking about them—or lots of things. But whatever it is, it is something you both love doing—and love doing together.

In fact, when we choose our partner, we are partly choosing him or her based on the connection we feel when we do certain things together—sailing, fixing houses, visiting art museums, traveling. Likewise, when we are searching for a way to connect to our stepchildren, we need look no further than the things we both like to do—skiing, playing video games, biking—and find more occasions to do them together.

Perhaps, like Anna and Michael, you realize there is no natural medium of connection between you and your stepchild. Then do a bit of thinking about which of his or her hobbies or interests you might genuinely enjoy learning about. The connection you create through this simple act will go a long way toward making your relationship stronger—and more fun.

# MAKE YOUR HOUSE
# THEIR HOME

No matter what the living arrangements are for your stepkids, at least some of the time they are living in your house. Help them feel as though it is their home too. Whether it is allowing them to decorate their rooms exactly how they want them, helping them find a private corner somewhere that can be all their own if they can't have a room of their own, or displaying photos, school drawings, or Father's Day presents, you want them to feel that this is one of the places on Earth that's "theirs," even if they aren't there all the time. It will go a long way toward making them feel wanted, a part of the family even when they are away.

Try to be sensitive to all the ways they could feel their space is violated. "One time, Bill's kids came for winter vacation. They had been at their mother's for two months straight. Their room doubled as our guest room and we had had guests. They arrived late at night and went straight to bed. The first thing in the morning, the two of them, age three and six, came solemn-faced into our bedroom. 'We have to talk to you about something,' they declared. 'Someone has been playing with our toys!' Even though two months had passed, they recognized that everything wasn't exactly as they left it and were upset."

It may not be possible for your stepchildren to have their own room, but you can think of creative ways for them to feel comfortable in your house. One child we know who lives half-time with Mom and half-time with Dad always travels with his tent, which they set up at whichever house he is in. That tent is what gives him a sense of home. Other kids always travel with special pillows or dolls or stuffed animals. The point is to make them comfortable.

Even if their room has to double as a guest room, let them be the ones to create the decorating scheme. (You can always explain to adult visitors if you are uncomfortable.) Again, it will create a sense of ownership that will help transform "your" house into "our" house. The more pleasant you make being with you, the more they will enjoy being there. And the more you will enjoy yourself too.

# PUT OUT THE WELCOME MAT

Your stepkids don't know if they're welcome in your home and in your life unless you tell them so. In their minds, the only person you're really interested in is their dad or their mom. Kids often feel like excess baggage because they sense that you're only trying to get along with them for the sake of peace in the household or to win the good graces of their parent. In their minds those reasons aren't good enough for them to make an effort to get along with you, let alone appreciate your positive attributes. To do that they'll need a bigger purpose, a personal incentive.

They need to know that not only are they welcome in the house but that you're welcoming them into your life. The only way they'll come to believe this is if you demonstrate your delight over and over again by telling them in a thousand and one ways how glad you are to have them around.

Welcoming a child into your life begins by simply putting a smile on your face, by being cheerful and good-natured. When you come together after they've been staying with the other parent say, "Hi, honey, glad to see you." Tell them, "I miss you when you're away." Ask them, "Will you sit down with me and visit for a minute?" Even if they don't sit with you right away, by asking, you're letting them know that you're interested. They'll see the efforts you're making.

Tell them, "I hope you had a good time at your mom's." Even if they don't respond outwardly, inwardly they'll feel thankful that you aren't competing with the other parent.

Be proud of your stepchildren by displaying their pictures around the house. Be sure to hang their artwork. Ask about their day, notice when they're feeling blue, ask how you can help, invite their friends for dinner. Show interest in their lives.

The transition from one house to the other is not always smooth. Think about what it's like when you have to pack your bags and stay somewhere else for a weekend. It takes time to get back into the groove. These transitions require special patience on your part, so don't expect that the kids can bounce from one house to another without adjustment time.

Don't ignore them even if they're ignoring you. Greet them warmly even if you don't feel it. No need to be gloomy just because the kids are suspicious of you. Wouldn't you be too, if a stranger was sleeping with your daddy or mommy? Why should they trust you? Don't push yourself on them.

Your stepchild needs lots positive attention from you. When you drop what you're doing they'll feel your genuine interest. If you're sidetracked and can't be bothered they'll get the message that you just don't care.

# CREATE SPECIAL TRADITIONS AND RITUALS

Part of what makes a family a family is special traditions—"We always have ham on Easter." "We always open our birthday presents *after* dinner." "We always go camping over the Fourth of July weekend." Part of what is lost when families break up is precisely these special little rituals that bring so much pleasure, especially to kids.

Now that you have a new family, it is time to create some rituals of your own. It's likely, particularly if the kids are older, that if you try to recreate traditions that they used to do, it will stir up too many old, painful memories. (But ask—maybe they would love to go caroling again the Sunday before Christmas.) You'll probably be better off with rituals that are unique to your new family, particularly since the kids are shuffling between parents over the major holidays. An annual Halloween party for all their friends, a special birthday dinner at a restaurant alone with you and your spouse, a sleepover with the four of you in the back yard every summer solstice—the possibilities are endless.

When establishing such traditions, remember to have patience. It isn't a tradition the first time around. You've got to do the same thing a few times at the proscribed occasion before the pattern is set and the true enjoyment sets in—which at least partially comes from remembering all the other times you've done this and sharing those stories together: Remember the time when we were in the tent and the dog was barking and Dad went outside in the dark and slipped on the dog poop and landed on his butt? Remember the time John ate all of Stephanie's birthday cake? Remember when Alice forgot to hard-boil the Easter Eggs and they broke all over the lawn?

Take care to include everyone in the family (although don't get too bogged down by party-poopers—they most likely will come around if you be sure to include some things you know they enjoy, like swimming or chocolate fudge) in the creation of the event: Tom, you be in charge of games because you're so good at that; Mom will handle the barbecue; Dan, you do the signs for the doors.

The more special times you create, the more love and laughter will invade your family—whatever its configuration.

# PAUSE BEFORE RESPONDING

This one could also be called "Duck When Emotional Shrapnel Comes Your Way." You know what we're talking about—those purposely mean little comments your stepkids lob your way just to get a rise out of you: My mother knows how to do laundry better than you (honest, this really happened); I hate your cooking; you are mean and ugly. The purpose of such remarks is to wound, to hurt you as much as they feel they have been hurt.

If you match them and react out of anger or fear, you are only escalating the cycle of pain. Rather, if you pause before responding, if you duck and let the emotional shrapnel fly over your shoulder, you will be in a place to ask the question: Why is this being said now?

The answer to that question might surprise you. You might figure out that Autumn and you have been getting along great recently, and she's feeling disloyal to her mother and seeking to put some distance between you. You might discover that Jason is flunking out of school and seeking to divert attention away from that fact. You might realize that you have been favoring your daughter over Julia in subtle ways, and she has a right to be upset. You might decide the best thing to do is ignore such a remark, teach Hollis how to cook for himself, or learn how to do laundry better.

But you will never figure out what's going on or come up with the best solution if you react instinctively to such baiting. No one can.

In certain elementary schools around the country, kids are learning impulse control using a traffic light as a metaphor. When someone hurts you, they are taught, the red light goes on. You stop, acknowledge how you feel to yourself—That hurts, I'm mad. Then the yellow light goes on. You think about all the ways you can respond—punch the person, call him names, walk away, tell him how you feel—and what the likely outcome of each of those will be. Then, green light, you choose the best option.

Seems to us that that's a useful formula for all of us any time we find ourselves in a heated situation.

# BE SENSITIVE TO
# EMOTIONAL BLACKMAIL

Your stepchildren have one great weapon to use against you—you are not their parent. And they will use it both in true anguish as well as to manipulate the situation to get what they want. Your job is to be able to differentiate between manipulation and a real problem, between blackmail and their honest feelings. While it can be difficult, this is not impossible. Again, it takes knowing the heart of the child and listening to your intuition.

"Michael was about four and was with us for the weekend," says Anna. "We had just gone to get donuts for breakfast and he had two. Well, he wanted another and we said no. So he proceeded to pitch a fit in the car, saying that he wanted to go back to his mother's because we were so mean. I knew that he loved being with his father and I knew this was just to test us, to see if we would give in and let him have a third donut. So I turned around in the seat to face him and said, 'The next time you say that you better really mean it because if you do, we will take you back to your mother's.' Not only did that stop him in his tracks then, but he never pulled that trick on us again."

Sometimes emotional blackmail needs to be ignored, sometimes it should be confronted head-on. If you pause before you react and consult your higher wisdom, you will be able to figure out what to do. But remember—not everything is emotional blackmail. Don't dismiss true cries as extortion. Context is everything.

"The times that Michael really cried for his mother were very different," recalls Anna. "I remember one in particular. His father was working and it was late at night and I heard sobs coming from Michael's room. He was about ten and had just begun living with us full-time. I went in and sat next to him and asked what was wrong. He said, 'I miss my mother. No matter where I am, I am always missing someone.' His plight touched my heart. As a person who grew up in an intact family, I never had to experience that longing for the missing parent no matter where you are. I held him for a long time, while he cried over the truth of his situation."

# STAY OUT OF SIBLING RIVALRY
## AS MUCH AS POSSIBLE

Kay has raised six children—two siblings from her first marriage, two stepchildren, and two children from her present marriage. Here's the bad news: "The kids fought a lot, picked on each other, and generally caused us misery," said Kay. But here's the good news: "The stepbrothers, who were the meanest to each other, have in their late twenties become the closest of friends," reports Kay. "We just wished they would have spared us the grief and gotten along when they were living at home," adds Kent. But there's more good and bad news: "Now that the kids are grown, they're close and they love to get together for family reunions at our house," says Kay. "Yup, they bring the nine grandkids, stay too long, and won't go home," teases Kent.

The most productive approach to sibling rivalry is: number one, stay calm; and number two, get their attention using humor. Nagging, begging, threatening, getting in the middle, or being the judge are techniques you've probably tried so many times that the kids mostly ignore you. The standard "You must be nice to your brother" is not an effective tool for soothing sibling rivalry. They've heard it before; besides, you probably don't have anything new to say on the subject either. Listing the advantages of getting along with each other is also not useful if no one is listening.

Take a deep breath and stay calm. Screeching and screaming only makes you look ridiculous. When you come unglued, the kids only pause long enough to wonder, "What's her problem?" When you're calm, get their attention using the silly, humorous approach. Jason said to his fighting six-year-old son and eight-year-old stepson, "Look, someone dropped dollar bills on the sidewalk." They looked and got caught up in the game of teasing him instead. Other times he jokes, "Oh, I see you're playing 'cats and dogs' again." Such pleasantry puts a less troublesome spin on the rivalry, making it more manageable for both kids and adults.

All kids, whether blood relatives or not, have strong ambivalent feelings toward each other. Letting kids know that it's normal to feel two ways about one another is helpful. Often they don't understand why they're fighting so much either. Jean said to her stepdaughter, "You care about her but right now you're so mad, you want her out of sight."

It's amazing that when you stay calm, the kids work out the most ingenious solutions. Four-year-old Molly and five-year-old Angie were in a tiff over the blue crayon and the coloring book. Mom said, "I see you both want to use the blue crayon and you both want to color the elephant. I think you can find a solution, let me know what you decide." In less than five minutes, the girls were coloring peacefully. "She gets to color the horse blue and I get to color the elephant yellow."

# SOLVE YOUR PROBLEMS
# WITH THEM DIRECTLY

No, they are not *your* children—but they are in your life and therefore you should strive as much as possible to deal with them directly, instead of appealing to their biological parents for help. You want them to see you as one of the adults in their lives whose advice they can benefit from and to whom they can come in times of need, and you can't create that kind of relationship if you are always running to your spouse whenever you have difficulty. To do so is to put yourself on their level—as a child—and place the biological parent over the two of you as the authority figure.

Instead, if you deal directly with them and use the bargaining power you already have, they will begin to realize that you must be taken into account. Sometimes as a stepparent you believe and behave as if you have no bargaining power. Here again you're tempted to look to your spouse for power and authority with the kids. No one can give you personal power, you have to find it within yourself and use what you have. You do have more inner power than you might think.

Lots of stepparents have trouble with this. They sit back and feel abused by their stepkids and resentful that their mate didn't step in to defend them.

Think about where your leverage is. Mark had a flexible work schedule and was willing to drive the kids to their many school activities and social commitments. As long as they were treating him well, he was good-natured, but if they gave him a rough time he wouldn't budge. "You wouldn't help me mow the lawn when I asked so I don't feel like driving you to your friend's house this afternoon." It didn't take long for the kids to learn that cooperating with their stepdad got them more of what they wanted than bucking him.

Think about what you do for the stepkids that is important to them. Do you iron their clothes, lend them your watch, chauffeur their friends, take them fishing, buy them treats? This is where you have power to gain their cooperation. Use your power lightly, without threatening, and you'll have a winning combination.

Will generously took Amanda to the store whenever she asked. "I'll meet you by the front door in thirty minutes," he said. Forty-five minutes later when she still hadn't shown up, he had her paged over the loudspeaker, "Amanda Ford meet your chauffeur at the information counter immediately." Since she didn't like being the focus of attention, that got her out of the store quickly! "Even though she was annoyed," recalled Judy, "I could tell by the slight twinkle in her eye that she had gained appreciation for the fact that she couldn't rattle him. She tested him often but eventually came to understand that he was in charge too, and if she wanted the goodies she'd have to respect his wishes."

# FINE-TUNE YOUR
# SENSE OF HUMOR

This can't be said enough—one of the most important keys to happy stepparenting is to laugh a lot—to yourself, with your mate, and with your stepkids.

"I used to use the 'wicked stepmother' thing a lot when the kids were young," says Anna. "I would say things like, 'Here comes the wicked stepmother to tell you it's time to clean your room,' or 'Here's the wicked stepmother arriving to say you've got to come in for dinner.' It played on the stereotype in such a way that we could all joke about it—and it was remarkably effective in getting them to do as I asked. Because I had called myself the name, they couldn't say it themselves—I usurped any power they might have tried to exert over me by making a joke of it. Because I teased about it, they couldn't take it seriously."

In order to brighten up the daily grind and have closer rapport with your housemates, be willing to laugh at yourself. Yes, it is easier to see the humorous side of your stepchildren and spouse than it is to stand back and see the crazy, immature things you do, but it's worth the effort. If you're willing to laugh at your peculiar little ways, there will be less wear and tear on your nerves.

Learning to laugh with your stepkids and spouse over mistakes and blunders gets things moving in a positive direction more quickly than a somber, serious approach. Laughing at our stepparenting foibles is a creative way, a less hurtful way of problem solving. It gives everyone renewed vigor for cooperating. Admit your blunders, but don't chastise yourself. "Yes, I was behaving like a wild woman last night," said Kate at the parenting group. "After I apologized we all had a good laugh. The next time I'm on the verge of screaming I'll warn the kids, 'Run for cover, the wild woman is taking over.'"

A playful atmosphere is good for all kinds of families; for step-families its an absolute necessity. Blended family life has many comical moments that you can use to turn stone-faced stepkids into chuckling participants. A few laughs a day will keep the stepparenting blahs from strangling the joy. If you can't think of anything funny, or when life is getting dreary, buy a laughing tape and play it as a surprise during dinner. Watch and see what happens.

# DESIGN AN "OUR GANG" ALBUM

W e highly recommend that you design a one-of-a-kind photo and story album to record the history of your expanded family. Just as there are wedding albums, baby books, and vacation albums, we think each stepfamily should have an "Our Gang" album depicting the significant events that makes your clan special. Include the description of your first meeting, record the names of all the relatives in your extended tribe, and display your album in a prominent place so everyone can see it. It's a testimony to your dedication and gives your stepfamily pride and team identification.

We suggest that you buy a scrapbook or a looseleaf notebook to collect treasures and souvenirs. The album, a memento that chronicles your life together, might include an expanded family tree listing *all* the relatives and steprelatives on *all* sides of the family. In drawing the family tree, don't leave anyone out. Even if you don't like them or don't have much to do with them, including them lets you and the kids see how all your lives are intertwined. It reminds everyone that there is no need to be afraid of skeletons in your closets. Another page might show in pictures and words the story of your first meeting, your favorite outing. List your likes and dislikes, your favorite colors, include everyone's little love-names.

Be sure to include plenty of pictures not only of special events like birthdays and Halloween, but of ordinary events such as the step-brothers playing catch together in the backyard, the kids doing chores, or Dad helping with homework. If the kids are old enough, give them a camera and ask them to take pictures of what it's like to be a member of this household.

Include pictures of the kids' biological parents too. Remember the biological parent has a permanent place in your stepchild's heart, so there is no need to stamp them out of the album. That page might be entitled, "Susie's Mother." A word of warning: Be sure to keep the titles upbeat; your stepchildren are highly sensitive to any put-downs of the other parent.

One page might be a statement of your goals: "We want to learn to get along," or "We want to go camping once a month." Write with colorful pens, cut out and paste in inspiring words from magazines to help you reach your goals. Ask the kids if they'd like to contribute. Don't coerce or push them, however. If you're cheerful about the project, they'll be sure to get interested in at least looking it over.

Regardless of what you call it, creating an album with a name, a logo, and a motto accentuates the unseen bond that keeps you hanging in. It's a playful portrayal that keeps you moving upward.

# WATER THE GOOD SEEDS

Vietnamese Buddhist monk Thich Nhat Hahn likes to use the metaphor of a garden when talking about the human personality. Each of us comes into adulthood with a handful of seeds (habits, patterns of feelings, ways of being) that we got from our parents. It is up to us to water the good seeds—seeds of love, compassion, kindness, understanding—so that they can blossom, and let the bad seeds—seeds of anger, despair, envy, fear, judgment—lie fallow. Otherwise we will reap a bitter harvest and pass on the bad seeds to our children.

Those of us who are parents are well aware that the anger and fear we chronically express has a way of showing up in the children in our lives. Many a child has stood between two parents begging them not to fight, only to see themselves saying and doing the exact same things in their adult relationships.

We reap what we sow. Therefore, if we want to live in a happy, loving family, we need to express as much love, compassion, understanding, and kindness to our stepchildren as we possibly can. In doing so, we not only water the good seeds in ourselves but in the children as well. The kinder we are to Lily and Joshua, the more they will learn kindness and live kindness. The angrier, more hostile, and dismissive we are to them, the more they will treat us that way too.

Remember—in planting a garden, there's no such thing as instant results. You have to water again and again before anything begins to emerge. And then the shoots are so tender that the slightest frost can kill them.

The same is true for the loving, tender seeds in our stepchildren. They need a lot of time and attention to grow well, a lot of patient tending. A bit of "frost" from you can do a great deal of damage.

So the next time you've been provoked into saying or doing something out of anger toward them, ask yourself what kind of harvest you want to reap. Water the good seeds in yourself and your stepkids, and your family will eventually become a garden of love.

# LOOK FOR THE
# UNSPOKEN "I LOVE YOU"S

Because our stepchildren may feel conflicted over positive feelings for us—they might feel disloyal to their other parent or resentful over the divorce (and "liking" us might be felt as approval of the split), to name just two reasons—they often have a hard time expressing feelings of love or affection. This can be very hard on us. After all, we pour out a great deal of attention, resources, affection, time, and care toward them—not to mention putting up with having our lives turned upside down—and get very little tangible in return.

In a wonderful book called *Girls Only*, Alex Witchel, a reporter for the *New York Times*, writes about being a stepmother, acknowledging that "you are always the third choice. No matter how much they like you, no one considers you an option for anything until Mom and Dad are unavailable first.... You're taken for granted because you can't be taken too seriously." Still, she points out, stepparenting can be marvelously satisfying and fulfilling, particularly if you look for the "unspoken 'I love you's.'" Because stepkids feel disloyal if they say "I love you" to a stepparent directly, you have to look for all the ways they do say it without words.

For Witchel, it is evident in the way her stepson slowed down to match her pace when she sprained her ankle, while her husband sprinted on ahead, oblivious to her inability to keep up. For Anna it was the way Michael always asked her to read his English and history homework. "He showed me that he knew I was a good writer and could help him." And it was evident in the way Zoe would come into the kitchen around dinnertime whenever she was staying over to ask Anna if there was anything she could do to help. For Erik, it was a letter Candice wrote to him apologizing for giving him a hard time. For Will, it was the way Amanda did her imitation of him. For Cynthia, it was the way her stepson would drape himself on the couch, with always a foot at least somehow touching her. For Margie, it was the way her stepkids would always want to talk to her too when they called home from college.

All of these are the precious rewards of our love and commitment, the sign language our stepkids use to acknowledge that we do matter in their lives. The more we look for such signs, the more we will feel the love that is in their hearts that may be too scary for them to express in any other way. They do care for us—be sure to take the time to notice how.

# WATCH FOR MIRACLES

Just because things might be rocky between you and your stepkids now doesn't mean they will always be that way. If you continue to act in a loving, lighthearted manner, as time goes on, you will become more and more part of their picture of the family. And sometimes, out of the blue, miracles happen.

"Michael was in high school, and we were almost completely alienated. It wasn't open warfare, just a tacit agreement to give one another a wide berth. I was feeling awful. I had been in this child's life for fourteen years, the last four of which he had lived with us full-time, and I felt that we weren't any closer than our first weekend together. I was out of town on a business trip and it happened to be Mother's Day. The phone rang at about 9:00 P.M. in my hotel room. 'I picked up the phone and it was Michael, just calling to wish me Happy Mother's Day.' I was so happy I cried."

Miracles do happen. The child who wished you would drop dead now considers you her best friend; the hostile boy who ignored you for years suddenly calls you Dad; your daughter and hers, who swore eternal enmity, are now running together for class office. You, who've never gotten along well with Joe, suddenly find him funny and entertaining.

Whatever is happening now is not an indication of what the

future will bring, particularly if we leave ourselves open to the possibility of the best outcome. The decision to open our hearts to the stepchildren in our care may need to be made over and over again as time goes by. But as long as we stay open, miracles can happen. The love that you are giving will come back to you somehow—if only in the shape of a child who majors in the same subject as you in college without ever realizing it was because they were so affected by your being in their life.

If you spend any consistent amount of time with a child, you will have a profound effect on who they are, and what matters to them in the world. Your existence in this child's life, this child who so "randomly" and "unintentionally" ended up with you, will help them become who they are meant to be. Isn't *that* miracle enough?

# NO MATTER WHAT, HOLD THEIR SOULS IN THE LIGHT

Above all, when things are rough, remember that these are young souls that have been entrusted to your care. You have a profound responsibility, a sacred duty, to help these souls blossom into their unique fullness. Even if today is full of argument and tension, you can hold the intention that tomorrow will be better and that these souls will find, with your help, the love and peace they are so hungry for.

Never underestimate the power of loving prayers to effect a good outcome. One prayer we like to say, especially when we are having trouble with someone, is called the "loving-kindness meditation." You start with yourself: may I be peaceful; may I be happy; may I be free from suffering; may I be filled with loving kindness. You then go to anyone you are having trouble with and offer them the same blessing: may Susie be peaceful; may Susie be happy; may Susie be free from suffering; may Susie be filled with loving-kindness. You then continue doing it for as many people as you want.

No matter what else is going on, the spiritual connection between us and our stepchildren is always there; when you pray, your souls will be linking up in some ineffable way. Even if it doesn't cause Susie to be nicer, we've noticed that it helps us to be nicer to Susie, which in turn ripples back to us.

Children come into our lives in many different ways—through birth; through adoption and fostering; and through stepfamilies. No matter how they got here, they are now a part of us and we a part of them. By a "twist of fate," your soul and the soul of your stepchild are now forever linked. When we acknowledge that link, when we see our task as caretaker of this budding soul, it is much easier to rise above the small stuff and focus on what truly matters. May we love them well—and may we have some fun in the process.

# Resource Guide

## STEPPARENTING

**Stepfamily Association of America**
215 Centennial Mall South
Suite 212
Lincoln, NE 68508
www.stepfam.org
800-735-0329

**Stepfamily Foundation**
333 West End Avenue
New York, NY 10023
(212) 877-3244
24-hour crisis line:
(212) 799-STEP

**The Joint Custody Association**
10606 Wilkins Avenue
Los Angeles, CA 90024
(310) 475-5352

**Positive Steps**
An online support group for
stepfamilies
www.postivesteps.com.

## WORK AND FAMILY ISSUES

**Families and Work Institute**
330 Seventh Avenue
New York, NY 10001
(212) 465-2044

**The Family Resource Center**
3041 Olcott Street
Santa Clara, CA 95054-3222

**Full-time Dads Newsletter**
http://www.parentsplace.com/rea
droom/fulltdad

Children's Rights Council
220 I Street N.E.
Suite 230
Washington, DC 20002-4362

SPECIFIC ISSUES
Exceptional Parents
For parents with disabilities
1 800-247-8080

National Information Center
  for Children and Youth with
  Disabilities
1 800-695-0285

Resource Center on Child Abuse
  and Neglect
63 Inverness Drive East
Englewood, CO 8012X
(303) 792-9900
800-227-5242

Momazons
National referral network for
  lesbian mothers
(614) 267-0193

MOMS Club
For at-home mothers
25371 Rye Canyon Road
Valencia, CA 91355

Mothers of Preschoolers
311 South Clarkson Street
Denver, CO 80210
(303) 733-5353

Mothers At Home
8310A Old Courthouse Road
Vienna, Virginia 22182
800-783-4666
E-mail: MAH@netrail.net

National Committee to Prevent
  Child Abuse
32 South Michigan Avenue
Chicago, IL 60604
(312) 663-3520
800-CHILDREN

American Anorexia/Bulimia
  Association
(212) 891-8686

National Association of Anorexia
Nervosa
(708) 831-3438

Family Violence Prevention Fund
800-313-1310

National Runaway Switchboard
800-621-4000

National Youth Crisis Hotline
800-448-4663

Rape, Abuse, and Incest National
Network
800-656-4673

Alcohol and Drug Helpline
800-821-4357

Cocaine Helpline
800-262-2463

National Clearinghouse for
Alcohol and Drug Information
800-729-6686

National Child Safety Council
Childwatch
800-222-1464

National AIDS Hotline
800-342-2437

Depression Awareness,
Recognition, and Treatment
800-421-4211

National Foundation for
Depressive Illness
800-245-4381

National Clearinghouse on Family
Support and Children's Mental
Health
800-628-1696

Planned Parenthood Federation of
America, Inc.
800-669-0156

## Books by Judy Ford

*Wonderful Ways to Love a Child*

*Wonderful Ways to Love a Teen ... Even When It Seems Impossible*

*Blessed Expectations: Nine Months of Wonder,*
*Reflection & Sweet Anticipation*

*Wonderful Ways to Love a Grandchild*

*Wonderful Ways to Be a Family*

For information on
Judy Ford's workshops and presentations write:
P.O. Box 834
Kirkland, WA 98083
425-823-4421

E-mail:
JFORDBOOKS@aol.com

Conari Press, established in 1987, publishes books
on topics ranging from psychology, spirituality, and women's
history to sexuality, parenting, and personal growth.
Our main goal is to publish quality books that will make a
difference in people's lives—both how we feel
about ourselves and how we relate
to one another.

Our readers are our most important resource,
and we value your input, suggestions, and ideas.
We'd love to hear from you—after all, we are
publishing books for you!

To request our latest book catalog,
or to be added to our mailing list, please contact:

CONARI PRESS
2550 Ninth Street, Suite 101
Berkeley, California 94710-2551
800-685-9595 • 510-649-7175
fax: 510-649-7190
E-mail: Conaripub@aol.com